PROF

Writing Matters

' 1999

PROFESSIONAL COMMUNICATION

Writing Matters

Alaine Hamilton

RIBA Publications

© Alaine Hamilton

Published by
RIBA Publications Ltd
Finsbury Mission, Moreland Street, London EC1V 8BB

ISBN 0 947877 08 8

Book design by Penny Mills

Typeset by Quorn Selective Repro Ltd, Loughborough

Printed by Billing & Sons Ltd, Worcester

Acknowledgments

I acknowledge with thanks contributions from Colin Campbell of Bickerdike Allen Partners to the Minuting and Reports sections; from John Clark of the Psychology Department at the University of Manchester who provided notes which I adapted for the sections about writing talks; and from Rod Males of the Department of Architecture at Manchester whose framework for an office manual is included in Section 8.

Any errors found in the book are my fault entirely. They are certainly not there for want of help and advice, which was generously given by many, including Bill Allen, Len Beaven, Stanley Cox, Joanna Fookes, Robert Johnstone, Nicholas Jones, John Timpson, John Veal, Oliver Willmore and George Young. I am very grateful to them all.

Last but not least, my thanks go to that well-intentioned wreaker of havoc, 'Anon', who toils on amongst us and to whom this book is affectionately dedicated.

A.H

Contents

Contents

List of Illustrations

Preface

If fate had been kinder, Inspector Clouseau might even now have been about to publish his memoirs. Asked for whom this undoubtedly memorable book had been written, he would probably have shrugged with Gallic opulence, paused for a moment of deep inner reflection and then pronounced: 'It has been written for everyone — and for no one.'

With less genius but possibly with more modesty, *this* book is aimed at architects in particular and professional practitioners associated with the building industry in general. Some of its readers may need much of the practical advice it offers, whilst others may use it as a book of reminders to be raided from time to time. But at whatever stage of career or level of practice they are, I hope that all its readers will find in it some food for thought. Bon appétit!

Alaine Hamilton
October 1988

FIG 1.0
A day in the life of . . .

I came down to a late breakfast. As usual, the kitchen floor was alive with dead cockroaches. I made some coffee and toast as I felt tired, although most mornings I feel like a boiled egg.

'What did you have for dinner?', I asked Sylvia.

'Nothing special', she said, 'I ate up the ham, and Polly the chicken.'

'The beagle's not very well', she added.

'If its nose is hot,' I said, 'you can give it fresh milk or boil it.'

After kissing and patting Sylvia and the beagle, I set off for work.

At eleven, I went to Bowers in the High Street and inspected the flashings on the roof which had blown off in the night before going back to the office.

Following a sharp attack of indigestion after lunch I went to survey a house in Cheam in a poor state of repair. Lifting the floorboards, dry rot was apparent. I thought I saw something dangling. [*It was a participle. Ed.*] I pointed out the condition of the marble fireplace to the client, very old and cracked. There was an old walnut piano in the drawing room which his wife played with intricately carved legs. I recommended a number of improvements, for better or worse.

When I got home, there was no sign of Sylvia and the house smelt of burnt milk and some kind of meat stew. The phone rang. It was the hospital saying they were admitting Sylvia with a surfeit of feathers.

And the moral to this sad story is: people who are good at communicating move up market and associate with corgis, not beagles. Or, to put it another way, it is possible to observe all the grammatical 'rules' and still fail to convey what you mean clearly and unequivocally. *It's the semantics that matter most.*

Introduction

'Average the fat generally that British too contains it's diet much accepted.'

A strange collection of words. If you were asked to try to sort them into a sentence, how would you begin? By trying to identify the verbs? *Contains*, and *it's* are obvious, but *accepted*, *diet* and *average* are also possible. Identifying the nouns is even more difficult, because *average* and *fat* could be adjectives and *diet* can be used in apposition to define another noun (as in *diet biscuits*).

Instead of seeking a grammatical solution, it is more likely that you would try to guess the semantics by spotting related pairs of words, probably starting with the obvious connection of *fat* and *diet*, *generally* and *accepted*, and *too* and *much*. Then you might ponder where *British* could go, and — *eureka*!

Similarly, have you ever stopped to consider how it is that we are able to understand Lewis Carroll's nonsense poem, *Jabberwocky*? Think of that first verse:

> ''Twas brillig, and the slithy toves
> Did gyre and gimble in the wabe:
> All mimsy were the borogoves,
> And the mome raths outgrabe.'

Most of the words are made-up nonsense items, but they are clearly identifiable as nouns, verbs, adjectives or adverbs. It is this categorisation that helps comprehension. For example, even though we have no idea what it looked or sounded like when the *mome raths outgrabe*, we are able to accept the possibility that a verb *to outgribe* exists in some mad dictionary somewhere, and that *outgrabe* is its past perfect.*

On the other hand, we would reject on purely semantic grounds a sentence with an adequate grammatical superstructure of words which is intellectually unacceptable such as *Dog is a god*, whereas *God is a dog* is a perfectly feasible notion – one which was quite familiar to the ancient Egyptians. So what does all this tell us about 'grammar'?

*Humpty Dumpty, who tiresomely knew everything about everything, later explained to Alice that *outgribing* is 'something between bellowing and whistling, with a kind of sneeze in the middle'.

Grammar – a new perspective

Most of us have mixed feelings about English grammar. We know intuitively that there is a framework of rules within which we must operate to communicate effectively – a kind of linguistic Plan of Work. In practice we often resist, ignore or modify its constraints to fit the needs of the moment. Unfortunately, this does not always have a happy result: we send out awkwardly phrased, ambiguous letters, reports, specifications and instructions more likely to confuse than enlighten. These curious items are viewed with particular dislike by those who hold the traditional view that 'grammar' is a prescribed set of nuts and bolts which fix the semantics firmly in place within a clearly defined linguistic framework.

It may be more constructive to see grammar as a *mechanism* which enables us to convert semantics (what we mean) into utterances (what we say or write). This mechanism is *part* of the linguistic framework which, far from being clearly defined, is a fuzzy, notional thing that derives from our innate ability as human beings to communicate. Superimposed upon it are the accumulated influences of the real world and, for some people, half-remembered remnants of tuition in English grammar, now an almost extinct ingredient of the school curriculum – although recently there have been several delegations of eminent *literati* to the Education Minister to plead for its reinstatement.

During the last three decades, the style of teaching and the content of the school curriculum have been influenced by various social, political and economic factors. Perhaps most significantly, the teaching profession's perception of its own role and importance has been challenged. Similarly, there has been a gradual change of attitude towards the use and function of language since modern linguistics became established as an academic discipline in the early 1960s and set about exposing the fallibility of the old prescriptive approach to teaching. For example, the editor of the *Oxford English Dictionary* now sees his job as 'reporting' rather than prescribing.

As a result of all this, many people find themselves trapped in a kind of linguistic no-man's-land between the everything-is-possible philosophy of modern language teaching on the one hand, and the stone-clad prescripts of formal English grammar on the other. Those whose favourite pastime is trying to identify 'good' or 'bad' grammar in present day written English can be forgiven their irritation at their lack of success when the existence, let alone the desirability, of grammar seems to be in question.

However, if we can accept the premise that grammar is a mechanism that enables us to express what we mean, it *can* be said to be 'good' or 'bad', depending upon whether or not it is functioning efficiently and enabling us to express what we mean, ie to communicate. Communication, on the other hand, can be described as good or bad according to whether or not it has succeeded. A successful communicator makes full and proper use of all the grammatical and lexical possibilities in the language so as to produce an attractive and effective result.

This success does not depend on all the grammatical 'rules' being observed, as Fig 1.0 shows.

Avoiding transgressions

The good/bad grammar myth persists because many writers are guilty of avoidable transgressions of what we could call grammatical etiquette, and this is what is traditionally referred to as 'bad grammar'. Ending a sentence with a preposition, failing to notice confusing juxtapositions, omitting essential punctuation and splitting infinitives are all regarded as examples of linguistic bad manners. They not only give an impression of carelessness and ineptitude but are also often thought to reflect a lack of intelligence.

So even for these rather negative reasons, there is a strong case for trying to avoid giving this kind of offence and for cultivating a critical approach towards what we write. A slapdash, poorly expressed letter of approach to a prospective client may well result in some exceptional opportunity being lost, whereas one that is clearly expressed, well reasoned, elegantly phrased and pleasingly presented will be read with interest and attention – and will get results.

Architects must also be able to describe adequately in words the concepts, functions and details presented in their drawings. A developer who knows little about architecture or building construction will search for something familiar by which to judge an architect as a professional person. His or her writing ability may be that crucial criterion.

Acquiring skills

Fortunately, the crafts, skills and techniques needed for effective writing can be acquired. Add to these a stringently self-critical attitude and the result is better communication and a significant improvement in the way a business operates. The purpose of this book is not only to reassure architects that such things are possible, but to persuade them that this is a pursuit worthy of their interest and attention. It will bring many rewards, personal as well as professional.

Writing Matters is in three parts. Part 1, which concerns the art and science of writing, is for leisurely and, it is hoped, pleasurable reading. Its philosophy and techniques underpin Parts 2 and 3, which are task- and topic-related. Two Appendices are included for the inquisitive of mind and stout of heart.

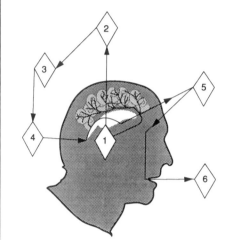

1 Idea!
2 Meaning (*semantics*)
3 Organisation (*notional grammar*)
4 Fine tuning (*formulation of utterance*)
5 Have I got it right? (*monitoring*)
6 Eureka! (*speech or writing*)

Diagram D1 – Communication in action

Part 1

Writing matters

Section 1

Style and approach

'Style is the dress of thought, a modest dress. Neat,
but not gaudy, will true critics please.'

(Samuel Wesley)

1.1 Formality:informality

'Style' can be understood in two ways. The first is in terms of a notional
scale of formality:informality. For example, Ray Cecil's style, familiar to
many architects through his regular articles in the *RIBA Journal*, can be
described as informal and fluent; the philosopher A J Ayer's as formal
and taut. (There is an example of Ayer in Appendix 1.) Both succeed,
in that they inform and instruct the reader, illuminate the subject
being addressed and are consistently targetted at a certain level of
readership. On a notional formality scale (see Fig 1.1) Cecil might be
at 5, Ayer at 9.

To be effective, communication must be appropriate to its context.
This means judging what amount of formality is suitable in the circumstances and selecting the right items from your verbal repertoire.

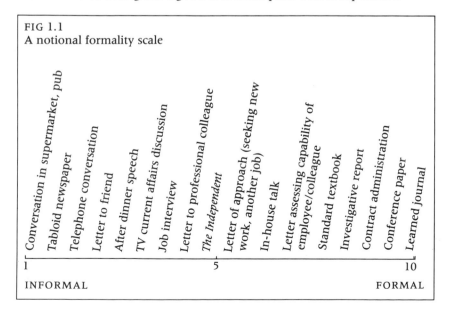

FIG 1.1
A notional formality scale

INFORMAL   FORMAL

17

On the whole, architects are friendly people who pride themselves on their approachability and lack of 'side'. However, it is often wise not to *Dear (first name)* anyone in a letter for the first time unless you are sure that this is appropriate. Your relationship could get off on the wrong foot. *Dear Ms/Mr* never offends anyone, and they may well respond *Dear Peregrine* anyway and (provided that's your name) all promises well. There's more on this subject in 5.1.

As far as clients are concerned, it is always better to use *Dear Ms/Mr*. Your relationship with the client is formal: he or she appoints and pays you according to the terms and conditions prescribed by your profession for providing an agreed service. It is very important to maintain a proper distance in business. There is always potential for embarrassment (at least) where a conflict of business and personal relationships could arise.

1.2 Styles of writing

'Dear Mr B--, Thank you for sending me your manuscript.
I will waste no time in reading it.'

(George Bernard Shaw)

The other way we understand style is as a way of writing that is characteristic of the author, one that reflects his or her view of life and events. Style in this case is the way the author chooses to express himself or herself. It can usually be identified whether or not the author's signature is attached to it. Biting wit and elegant turns of phrase typify the writing of George Bernard Shaw, powerful narration and compelling rhetoric that of Winston Churchill.

A 'characteristic' style can also be fabricated. Clive James' is an example. Watching him on television you become almost breathless trying to follow the twists and turns of syntax and epigrammatic sleights of hand. The style is slick and apparently witty. If you had time to analyse what the man is *saying* (or to read one of his books) you might be disappointed. Neat, certainly, but distinctly gaudy.

Style is also reflected in the way we use words. The legal profession is notorious for the opacity of its terminology – as lawyers might express it. *You* might say that legal language is hard to understand. That is because you are not a lawyer; *they* understand it. Unless lawyers specialise in construction litigation, they may not understand *you* when you talk about U-bends, U-values, dpcs, dpms, sulphate attacks and masonry bees. Most professionals have their own special verbal repertoire of terms that is only understood by insiders. These vocabulary differences are often disparaged as 'jargon'.

1.3 Jargon

Jargon is like bad breath: it's something that you notice about *other* people. Speakers or writers mindlessly churn out idioms and terminology which are familiar to members of their own trade or profession but meaningless to everyone else. Apart from the intended message being unintelligible, there is also the danger that the writer or speaker who uses ready-packaged phrases and ideas may not have taken the trouble to think through problems properly or evaluate situations in a real context.

In fact, we all have our jargons. They can be connected with our hobbies and interests, as well as the way we earn a living. Listen to the conversation of anglers, farmers, stamp collectors or dog breeders. What, for instance, do you expect to do with a Large White? Dangle it from the end of a line, or take it for a walk, or stick it in an album next to a Penny Black?*

These special codes and terminologies are traditionally part of the way groups maintain their identities, communicate speedily and precisely and keep their skills safe from marauding outsiders. Newspaper headlines are particularly interesting: not only do they use a vocabulary that seems to have been exhumed from some bygone age (SPANIARD IN BID TO SLAY WINDMILL) but they manipulate – some would say torture – language into text that has to be squeezed into a column format. As a result, they have developed their own species of grammar as well as an individualistic lexicon, to the extent that instead of being artful 'read-me's, they become virtually unintelligible. The three following examples are from *The Guardian*.

MINISTER'S WORKSHY APOLOGY
LAW IS URGED TO CONTAIN A KITCHEN THREAT
BANANA SKIN ROLE FOR WHITELAW

So when you are writing to people outside the building industry – and these are often your prospective clients – remember that they may be

*It's a pig.

19

completely unfamiliar with the terminology of architecture and building construction. If you want a project to go well, make sure that they *do* understand your letters, reports, drawings and specifications.

To sum up, jargon is not *intrinsically* bad; it evolves and exists for understandable reasons connected with professional or group survival. The trouble is that words or phrases are abstracted from, say, medical terminology (such as 'traumatic', 'terminal') and are used in other contexts where they are not valid. As a result, they take on a separate, weaker meaning which has little or nothing to do with the original. Eventually they become lexical fakes – sometimes freaks.

1.4 'Correct usage'

Language does not stand still; it is a moving target, a kaleidoscope of continually shifting items that form patterns momentarily and then disperse and reassemble in other formations. Changes in sound, meaning and syntax go on all the time. Therefore he who prescribes the 'correct' usage of words treads treacherous ground. At the same time, as discussed in the Introduction, the marshlands of linguistic bad manners have to be negotiated in the real world of business.

It is about as much use trying to resist linguistic change as trying to turn back the tide; the best we can hope for is to develop an awareness of what's going on. The theme that can be observed to run consistently through literature from its earliest surviving remnants is that the younger generation are a lot of no-goods who are misusing and corrupting the beloved mother tongue, and that as a result the country is going down the drain. There is always resistance to change.

So what is meant by correct usage? A writer or speaker uses words according to his or her understanding of what is correct at a particular point in time, but the receiver of the utterance in question may have some other understanding of correctness because of difference in age, education, social background and profession. This suggests that correctness is largely a matter of subjective judgment. All right, you say, but surely there is some middle ground? Yes, of course there is, for if there were not some degree of consensus, communication would be impossible. Deciding the parameters of that middle ground is as difficult as trying to define a linguistic framework, but we have to try. That is why this book homes in on a few commonly accepted problem areas (see the next Section), but otherwise considers more general aspects of style and the crafts needed to become better at writing English.

Other books are available which discuss the historical niceties of word usage, for example the well-known *Complete Plain Words* by Sir Ernest Gowers. The latest (1986) edition has an interesting section on the subject, but the book's revisers are clearly aware that the ground is fast slipping away from under their feet.

So, to avoid sinking without trace in the linguistic morass and to get one foot at least firmly planted on that middle ground, you will need to 'tune in' to language, observe the way it is used by others, and be critical of the way you use it yourself.

'When *I* use a word,' Humpty Dumpty said in a rather scornful tone, 'it means just what I choose it to mean — neither more nor less.'

(Lewis Carroll)

Section 2

Knotty problems

2.1 Units of communication

The hierarchy of basic units of communication in written English is shown in this diagram.

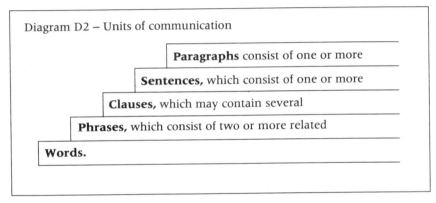

Diagram D2 – Units of communication

Paragraphs consist of one or more
Sentences, which consist of one or more
Clauses, which may contain several
Phrases, which consist of two or more related
Words.

THE PARAGRAPH
One or more sentences that make up a complete unit of thought.
Short paragraphs help comprehension, especially where the subject matter is difficult to grasp. Material also *appears* more digestible if it is presented in smallish lumps. There is nothing more off-putting than to be faced with a whole page of unrelieved running text. Written information should be allowed to 'breathe', with plenty of white space around it.

THE SENTENCE
One or more clauses that together make up a coherent grammatical and syntactical entity.
Recent research has shown that the average sentence in written English consists of 18 words (like this one).

THE CLAUSE
A main clause and/or its subordinate clauses.
The most important item is given in the main clause (ie 'new' information); further or 'given' information in the subordinate clause(s).

EXAMPLES:

(a) *John died from eating an apple, which became stuck in his throat.*

You can't subordinate the 'John died' clause and make sense.
You have to *coordinate* it:

(b) *An apple became stuck in John's throat and he died.*

THE PHRASE
A group of related words.
These may be adverbial *(on the following Friday)*, prepositional *(to the edge of the cliff)*, genitive/possessive *(Mary's brother and sister)* etc.

THE WORD
Single units that make up phrases.
The right choice of words to reflect the semantics is crucial. A collection of the words of a language is called a lexicon.

Putting it together

A great deal of mystique has always attached to defining and analysing 'the sentence', as if it were the centre of the linguistic universe. In practice, what is important is the way we manipulate *clauses*: how we relate them one to another, how we weight them, how we order them. This is what puts light and shade into our writing. The art is to make grammatical relations match semantic relations. However, whilst short sentences are generally easier to understand, a series of single-clause sentences is distinctly tedious. When we were very young, we wrote letters like that.

'Dear Mum, Hope you are well. I am. I had sausages for dinner again. The cat fell in the dishwasher. Granny says see you soon please god. Love Peregrine'

2.2 Punctuation

The function of punctuation is to help comprehension; too little of it can be as confusing as too much. Punctuation is necessary in some places and desirable in others. Full stops, colons and semi-colons help to structure sentences; commas help to separate words and ideas within sentences. Only three items of punctuation are needed in the first example below, a long but well-constructed sentence: one colon and two commas. In the second, one comma is *desperately* needed.

EXAMPLES:

(a) *When you are trying to appraise the acoustics of a concert hall the first and most difficult consideration is to decide whom you should believe the people who prove their satisfaction by buying their own tickets the press who have been provided with complimentary tickets but are burdened with the professional necessity as they see it of having to write something relatively sensible or the surveys carried out by various researchers.*

(b) *Monica walked on the top of her head just visible above the hedge.*

Whereas commas tend to be over-used, full stops are generally under-used. (James Thurber once wryly commented that this is the Century of the Comma Man. And Woman, one must hastily add.) The longer a sentence, the more mental effort is needed to sort it out and understand it. Oscar Wilde's epigrammatic style demonstrates the effect of the short, sharp utterance:

'All women behave like their mothers. That is their tragedy. No man does. That's his.'

Not everyone understands the differing functions of colons and semi-colons. A colon usually indicates that something is going to follow: a list of items, for example. Don't use a dash after a colon; it's unnecessary.

As you can see from the two sentences you have just read, the semi-colon is used to create a break when the following clause is a continuation of the idea contained in the first part of the sentence, whereas the colon has a distinctly anticipatory function. Semi-colons are also used to separate listed items or clauses, and (a), (b), (c) etc options. In specifications, use colons for expressing ratios, such as in gradients (1:6) and mixes (1:2:6), rather than writing 'one in six', 'one part cement to two parts sand', etc.

However, there are times when no amount of punctuation can rescue a poorly constructed sentence.

'He has bought a Wiltshire millhouse to go with his Mayfair residence, where he is learning to fish.'

(Respected periodical)

Rephrase *To go with his Mayfair residence he has bought . . .* and you don't need any punctuation at all; the meaning is clear (if not so intriguing!).

2.3 The split infinitive

'A verb has a hard time enough of it in this world when
it's all together. It's downright inhuman to split it up.

(Mark Twain)

Inhuman or not, in speech we often split infinitives, and it is argued that this is because it feels more 'comfortable' and natural, and that grammatical effort is needed to avoid splits. In writing, and in business correspondence in particular, we have to be more prudent. The argument rages on, especially in the columns of *The Times*, and whether or not we have strong feelings on the subject, we need to find á way of living with it in the real world. Architects are used to finding pragmatic solutions, whether to suit the client's needs, or because funds are running out, or for reasons of buildability. So here is some pragmatic advice.

First,
make sure you know what a split infinitive is. It's where the infinitive of a verb (eg *to love, to hate*) is 'split' by an intruding word or words (eg *to dearly love, to intensely hate*). Sometimes it is split by a large chunk of material, as in Councillor Bluff's example on page 28.

Second,
check through your own letters and reports to identify any splits.

Third,
to avert the possible wrath of the recipient, consider the best way of 'correcting' them.

There are three ways of approaching the problem:
(1) See if you can remove the intruding word (usually an adverb), eg 'to completely re-design the building'. If the meaning stays the same, it wasn't needed anyway; you have simply done a useful bit of pruning.

(2) If the meaning requires the word to remain, eg 'We intend to immediately brief the services engineer', consider whether you can transpose the intruder to some other position in the clause or sentence. Siting an adverb *before* the infinitive is rarely satisfactory because adverbs typically affect the meaning of the whole clause, not just the infinitive. For that reason they are usually best sited at its end, eg 'We intend to

brief the services engineer immediately'. The alternative 'immediately to brief' is unacceptably awkward anyway.

(3) If neither (1) nor (2) can resolve the situation, ie the meaning is changed by omission or transposition, or the resulting clause or sentence is awkward, then consider rephrasing (see examples (a) and (b) below). Rephrasing means that you have to expend some effort and use up a little of your valuable time. It's worth it in the long run.

Perhaps it will throw some light on the split infinitive argument if we consider *why* people object to splits so vehemently. It may be that their attitude is conditioned by the remnants of a Classics-based education. In Latin, the infinitive is just one word – for instance, *amare* (to love). Therefore the anti-split lobby contends that the *to* is an undetachable part of the infinitive construction. However, ancient Latin was very different from its remote descendant, modern English: it was a precise, compressed language* with a relatively limited lexicon, whereas English has a vast and diverse lexicon which reflects the influences of many different languages and cultures and therefore has a predisposition towards grammatical irregularity.

At least there is some logic in the Latin grammar argument. There are probably many more people who confidently assert that split infinitives are unacceptable without any good reason except that they 'feel' that splitting is 'wrong'. In fact, they are unlikely to so much as *notice* a split infinitive if they are in tune with what the writer is saying or if he or she is a friend or colleague. Where the writer–reader relationship is adversarial or competitive, it's quite another matter; such linguistic indiscretions are seized upon with great glee and broadcast without mercy.

Did you spot the split infinitive in the paragraph above? If you didn't, it was because your eye was drawn to the italicised *word* and your brain forgot to check the grammar. Here's another teaser.

Q When is a split infinitive not a split infinitive?
A When it's not a grammatical split.

Consider the next examples, where *really* and *clearly* are apparently intruding adverbs.

A famous puzzle for Latin translators is Tacitus' comment about the emperor Galba, whom he described as capax imperii, nisi imperasset. *A possible translation of these four words is that (Galba) had in theory the capability of being a ruler, if only he hadn't in the event been called upon to be one — and been found to be* incapable' (28 words).

EXAMPLES:

(a) *I want you to clearly understand what I am saying.*

(b) *I want you to really consider my proposal.*

The first rule in linguistic detective work is to ask: What does the evidence *mean*?

(a) means
I want you to understand exactly what I mean when I say that . . .

Clearly has disappeared. In this context it is meaningless: it is up to the *speaker* to provide the clarity needed for the understanding to take place.

(b) means
I want you to consider my proposal fully and seriously.
There is no suggestion that the proposal or the consideration is *un*real, so *really* has got nothing to do with the *meaning*. (We shall see in a minute what it is *really* doing.)

So, failure to select appropriate words – perhaps it could be called lexical laziness – is one cause of split infinitives. The examples also demonstrate another.

In much the same way as jargon words at first seem striking and innovative and then gradually weaken with over-use, some over-worked adverbs have lost their powerful adverbial function in the syntax and are often used simply as lexical highlighters. For example, *really* is a handy word that we have all used for emphasis since our earliest days ('Mum, I'm *really* hungry', 'Dad, I *really* hate school/want a Porsche for my birthday'). In speaking, *really* is often used as an alternative for *very* or *very much*. In this emphasising role, it is just as likely to pop up in the middle of an infinitive construction as anywhere else because, used as a qualifier, *really* always precedes what it is qualifying. There is no question of its being shifted to some other position in the clause.

Another important rule in the science, as opposed to the art, of writing or speaking, is to test how words function.

EXAMPLES:

(c) *I want you to sing loudly.*

Loudly is an adverb of manner answering the question *How do you want me to sing?* It qualifies the verb and must follow it. No one would contemplate saying *I want you to loudly sing.*

(d) *I want you to really consider my proposal.*

Now to test *really*. Can you place it after the verb like *loudly*? No. Why not? Because it is not *functioning* as an adverb; it is a lexical addition, an importee introduced for emphasis. It has nothing to do with *grammar*.

(e) *I want you to sing really loudly.*
There it is again, but this time it is qualifying a 'real' adverb.

Fortunately, there is some solid ground which we can tread with more confidence. Most people, whatever their educational background and chosen profession, would agree that *gross* splits are ugly and should be avoided at all costs.

EXAMPLE:
Councillor Bluff said he wanted to, *amongst other things, one of them being the cost of the chairman's Rolls Royce and another being the question of Mr Harty's recent holiday in the Bahamas – to say nothing of Mr Grinsdyke's travel expenses, especially those connected with his 'niece' in Paris,* propose *a review of directors' emoluments.*

Finally, it is important to try to keep a sense of proportion. Split infinitives may be intensely irritating to some people but, unlike many of the linguistic undesirables considered later in Part 1, they are essentially only awkward transpositions and seldom lead to confusion or misinformation. Those are the real cardinal sins in the context of communication. By comparison, split infinitives are harmless, if emotive, hiccoughs.

POSTSCRIPT
It may interest readers who revere all things Classical that in *modern* Greek there is *no* infinitive construction. For example, *I must go* is written as *I must I go* – that is, the present indicative is used instead of the infinitive.
　　Perhaps the earthquakes that periodically devastate the Aegean islands in these modern times are simply the shock waves of millions of ancients turning over in their graves.

'. . . that was in the Olden Days, when the Romans were top nation on account of their classical education.'

(Sellars and Yeatman)

2.4 Confusing conjunctions

And, or, but, nor, neither are all coordinating conjunctions in their own right. Some of them are also used in pairs.

'And' and 'but'

There is some confusion about how to use the conjunctions *and* and *but*. Their conventional function is to coordinate clauses, and the best way to understand how they work is to consider some examples.

EXAMPLES:
(a) *He learnt to ride a bicycle and often fell off.*
(b) *He learnt to ride a bicycle* but *often fell off.*

Example (a) is a simple statement. It is accepted that bicycle riders often fall off. In (b) there is an element of surprise that he still fell off in spite of having learnt how to ride a bicycle. Example (a) has no particular emphasis; example (b) has.

Similarly
(c) *She is pretty and he is ugly.*
(d) *She is pretty* but *he is ugly.*

Example (d) has a surprise and is 'marked' (has emphasis). In example (c) *and* simply coordinates two contrasting observations. The emphatic effect is more obvious when you repeat the examples out loud.

To sum up, *but* denies or corrects the clause that precedes it. It highlights its own clause at the expense of the previous.

It is often said that neither *and* nor *but* should be used to begin a sentence. On the contrary, it is commonly done for dramatic or emphatic effect.

'A building is a sign, expressing its purpose through its form . . . . In some buildings, such as a garage or a storage shed, expressive quality is exhausted at this level. But a house may also be a home, giving it a deeper, symbolic level of meaning.'

(Peter F Smith)

And can be used at the beginning of a sentence to draw special attention to an additional point you wish to make. It is essentially a rhetorical device, one of many linguistic tricks used by politicians (refer to Appendix 1 to see how Mrs Thatcher uses it).

'There are lies, damned lies, and statistics. And public
expenditure white papers of the sort published yesterday.'

(The Guardian)

The old adage about never beginning a sentence with *and* or *but*
became redundant long ago as their function as basic coordinators
developed into a powerful emphatic device. But(!) remember that the
effect of any focusing device is neutralised if you use it too often. Keep
such tricks for special linguistic occasions.

'Either', 'or', 'neither', 'nor'
These four conjunctions can be used singly to coordinate clauses
or in pairs of *either . . . or, neither . . . nor*.

EXAMPLES:
(a) *You can come on Friday, or wait until Monday.*
(b) *His omelettes are not light enough, nor are his soufflés.*
(c) *I like neither tea nor coffee.*
(d) *Peregrine likes an egg for breakfast, either boiled or scrambled.*

Example sentence (e) needs some correction. Any suggestions?
(e) *Never break your bread or roll in your soup.*

You may have tried to replace *or* with *nor* and found that it didn't work.
As usual, the key to the solution is in the semantics, not the grammar
– what does the sentence *mean*, rather than what does it *say*.

So you might insert a pair of commas:
(f) *Never break your bread, or roll, in your soup.*

Alternatively, you could reinstate *your* before *roll*. The word is
there in the semantics; it was dropped when the sentence came to
be uttered. Language is full of 'invisibles' of this kind, because we
instinctively try to get rid of redundant words and phrases as we
go along. Our utterances would otherwise be repetitive and boring.
However, confusion can arise from this intuitive pruning procedure
(known as *ellipsis* in the linguistics business) if words that are crucial
for proper comprehension by the receiver are omitted. *Only leave out
words, phrases or clauses if the meaning stays the same without them.*

2.5 Perplexing pronouns

'I' or 'we'?
In formal letters, always use *we*. It may seem odd if you are truly a

sole practitioner, but it is sound advice (also see 5.4). No one will really confuse you with Royalty, who abandoned *we* a long time ago to seek refuge in *one*, which has been just as troublesome. There is much to be said for being a commoner and having no doubt about whether one is singular or plural.

You can use *we* as a persuasive device when you are trying to draw someone into your way of thinking. Another use is when you want to avoid giving the impression that you are being critical; *we* is an effective way of establishing a common cause with the reader.

Conversely, use *I* and *you* when you *want* to create a divide. Refer again to Appendix 1 and see how Margaret Thatcher introduces *we* towards the end of her party political broadcast to gather up the electorate and unite them into voting for her.

'He' and/or 'she'?

It offends the sexist-sensitive to use *he* when *she* is just as appropriate. However, difficulties tend to arise when we are expressing generalities – for example, in practice manuals. As discussed in 11.3, using the plural *architects* results in the compromise *they* and avoids the issue, but it sometimes inhibits a writer's style and makes it awkward. The *Architect's Job Book* refers to the architect as *he*, because it is referring to the professional or contractual *role* of the architect. The same happens with the JCT standard forms of building contract.

It is nonsense to contend that if only we got our terminology right, society would be miraculously transformed. As Peter Trudgill remarked in *Sociolinguistics* (1974):

'Linguistic changes follow social changes very readily;
but it is not always a simple matter to make them *precede*
social changes'.

However, remembering to write *he or she*, even though we already solidly support the principle of sexual equality, may serve as a reminder to the less enlightened that there is still room for improvement.

Missionaries in the field have taken to inventing neuters such as *chairperson, draughtsperson* and *foreperson*. (There have even been advertisements for a *Person Friday*.) It is a beguiling pursuit.

'Lot 123: a 19th century mahogany tallperson with
crossbanded drawers'.

Probably smelling strongly of mothparts.

'Which' or 'that'?

Like *and* and *but*, it all depends on the way *which* and *that* are made to function. *Which* can function as an interrogative pronoun (*Which hat shall I wear?*), and *that* as a conjunction (*I know that my Redeemer liveth*). In addition, *which* and *that* can introduce relative and subordinate clauses.

EXAMPLES:
(a) *The hat* [which hat? The hat] *Mary was wearing was blue.*
This is a *relative* clause. It defines a noun. You can use *which* or *that*, or leave them both out.

(b) *The hat, which* [what happened to it? It] *blew off his head in Brixton, was later found at Blackfriars.*
This is a *subordinate* clause. It adds information. You can use *which* or *that*, but you *must* use one of them.

Note also the difference in the hidden questions, and the pair of commas which typically demarcates a subordinate clause.

(c) *This is the cat that* [What did it do? Information: It] *ate the rat that* [What did it do? Information: It] *lived in the house* [Which house? Definition: The house] *(that) Jack built.*

The first two clauses are subordinate, the third is relative.

2.6 Spelling

This is where you are on your own. If you spell badly your friends will pity you and your enemies rejoice in your downfall. There is no rescue at hand in the shape of new perspectives or interpretations, but it may be some comfort to know that insistence on correct spelling is relatively recent and is largely due to the influence of such as Dr Johnson. There wasn't even a published English dictionary until the early seventeenth century. However, back in the problematical present there are always plenty of excuses offered for poor spelling. Here are a few:

Medical insensitivity
'There's a lot of mild dyslexia about. Only the severe cases ever come to light.'

Educational depravity
'My English teacher was awful.'

32

Occupational heredity
'My dad's a jernalist and you know how bad they are at spelling.'

Continental duplicity
'Foreigners don't have proper languages of their own, so they use ours and confuse our spelling.'

Diet deficiency
'Nanny never let me eat enough fish and my brain got starved.'

Because English has a more extensive lexicon than any other language, we have the advantage of a marvellous choice of words at our disposal but only a distant prospect of being able to spell them all. At the same time, in our everyday language we use a relatively small number of them – more, of course, in writing where the thinking time available is greater.

So, if spelling is a problem, what can you do about it? If you had the time, you could read more books, do crosswords, study a foreign language. All these things make you more particular about getting words right. And unless you are too word-blind to make it out on the bookshelf, there is always the dictionary. However, as you are bound to be short of time and unenthusiastic about going on a fish diet, perhaps electronic assistance is a solution.

If you own or have access to a personal computer, the software often includes a spelling check facility. This is useful anyway in tracking down typographical errors, such as transposed letters, which can afflict the best of spellers. If your spelling is wildly out, the spell check may offer alternative words, and whatever you do, don't accept these blindly. The vital difference between the pc and the human brain is that the pc has no sense of context; all it can do is offer similar letter patterns from a limited list of alternatives.

'Foreigners always spell better than they pronounce . . .'.

(Mark Twain)

Section 3

How to improve your writing style

Probably the most useful piece of advice to anyone who wants to improve his or her writing style is to rephrase rather than write down something that is 'correct' but uncomfortable. George Orwell said: 'A scrupulous writer . . . will ask himself . . ."Have I said anything that is avoidably ugly?"'. We need to use language in a flexible and responsive way to generate effective and attractive communication.

3.1 Be crisp, clear and concise

Aim for a clear, direct and economical style. Writers who are anxious to inform or explain or persuade often use long and complex sentence constructions, too many clauses, and superfluous words and phrases.

Directness and economy usually go hand in hand. On the 'Today' programme, Dr Caroline Jackson, the Wiltshire Euro-MP, declared her intention of putting down a resolution against 'Eurospeak'. She quoted some startling examples of bureaucratic gobbledegook, such as a 'negative reserve', meaning a deficit, and a 'retrospective advance', which was something to do with budgetary matters. The pearl in the linguistic pudding was a translation of the saying 'out of sight, out of mind' into German. A miracle of misinterpretation produced 'an invisible maniac'.

3.2 Root out repetition

```
Enclosed is a copy of a self-explanatory letter today
forwarded to the local authority, which is self-
explanatory.
```
(Anon)

Writers repeat themselves because they are unsure that they have managed to get the message across. Giveaways are redundant phrases such as 'As I said earlier,' or 'To restate the position,' 'I think I'm right in saying', even 'It cannot be said too often . . .'. It *can*! A message that is clearly and concisely expressed won't need repeating until it is time to sum up.

Using different words to say the same thing is a common fault and is not as easy to detect. The result is a weak 'wordy' style which quickly becomes tedious.

EXAMPLE:
When we are uncertain whether we have managed to get the message across we tend to repeat ourselves, because we are not sure that we have been able to make ourselves understood in the first instance.

'He multiplieth his words without knowledge.'

(*Job 35.16*)

3.3 Watch for ambiguities

```
Please carry out internal doors and some external doors
as shown on drawings ...
```
(Anon)

It is often hard to spot ambiguities in your own writing. Unfortunately, they are usually abundantly obvious to others, and this is where it helps if a colleague will agree to be your reader. Ambiguity can arise from words being wrongly used or misplaced, or clauses put into confusing juxtaposition. For example in Fig 1.0:

'I . . . inspected the flashings on the roof which had blown off in the night . . .'.

The reader is not sure whether it is the flashings or the roof which has blown off – or both, come to that.

Letters and instructions should be scrupulously checked to make sure that there is no potential for misinterpretation. If there is, a time-consuming flow of letters asking for clarification may follow or, should the worst happen, a period of deafening silence followed by a letter from the addressee's solicitor.

```
        SPECIAL TODAY!

Small Businesspersons lunch

    Half fresh Greapfruit
    Battered Place & chips
       Choice of tarts
```

Just the place to break your bread or roll in your soup.

3.4 Avoid generalities . . .

```
Most blocks of flats have condensation problems ...
Pitched roofs always perform better than flat ...
```
(Anon)

Sweeping statements that are unsupported by evidence should be avoided, especially in reports (see 7.5), which are essentially specific. They are not likely to contribute anything interesting or original to what you are saying and seldom stand up to analysis.

The introduction to a recent important research report blandly stated 'The main reason for constructing a building is to keep the rain out'. Quite so . . . no, wait a minute!

Q   *Why are you building this building?*
A   *To keep the rain out.*
Q   *To keep the rain out of what?*
A   *Out of the building . . . I am going to build . . . Oh dear . . .*

It could be said that the main *function* of a building is to keep the rain out (and keeping the rain out could arguably be the main *problem* in designing it). The main *reason* for constructing a building is usually not unconnected with the fact that one party has contracted another party to do so!

. . . and euphemisms . . .

Euphemism is a flowery and pedantic mode of expression and should not be used in business correspondence. Apart from often appearing ridiculous, it leaves room for misinterpretation. Say what you mean. A building that is about to fall down is about to fall down; it is not 'imminently prone to entropic disintegration'. Even if you are terrified of your secretary, it is better to point out a few typing errors rather than 'indicate sundry digital infelicities'.

. . . or lexical confusion may result

'Lexical confusion' is a euphemism for using the wrong word. This tends to happen where two words resemble one another but mean different things. The pairs given below are notorious* lexical Black Spots.

AFFECT/EFFECT:
To *affect* is to have an effect upon something.
To *effect* is to bring about or accomplish something.

*One of the BBC weather men often used to refer to *notorious frost hollows* until someone, probably with a vested interest, told him that *well-known* might be more suitable.

36

COMPLIMENTARY/COMPLEMENTARY:
A *complimentary* remark is made by someone who tells you that you are wonderful. They may even give you a *complimentary* (ie free) ticket to the opera.
Complementary means completing. Where one thing *complements* another, the result is completeness.

DEPENDENT/DEPENDANT:
Dependants (noun) are people who *depend* upon you; they are *dependent* (adjective).

DISCREET/DISCRETE:
Discreet means tactful, prudent.
Discrete means separate, distinct.

ENTAIL/ENSUE:
Apart from a special meaning connected with settling estates, *entail* means to impose, necessitate.
Ensue means to happen afterwards.
The agreement *entailed* a long series of discussions/a long series of discussions *ensued*.

FARTHER/FURTHER:
Farther is when something is more distant.
Something *further* is something additional.

INFER/IMPLY:
Infer is to deduce from facts or information given.
Imply means to signify, insinuate.
You might *infer* something from a letter; a letter might *imply* something.

LATE/LATTER/FORMER:
Latter means following another, or the second of two mentioned items.
Latterly means towards the end of a period, or of late.
A train as well as a deceased person can be *late* (but the *latter* can only be *very* late whilst still alive). Someone who was *lately* your husband was recently your husband. If you divorce him, he will become your *former* husband. *Latterly* he may have been your husband, but *formerly* he may have been something quite different.

LEAD/LED:
Led is the past perfect of the verb *to lead*. Peregrine might be *led* astray

by the beagle pulling on its *lead*. The Beloved *Leader* of your firm may have feet of clay, but certainly not feet of *lead*.

PRACTICE/PRACTISE:
When you *practise* (verb) architecture, you can be said to be in architectural *practice* (noun). The same verb/noun distinction applies to *license/licence*.

PRINCIPAL/PRINCIPLE:
A *principle* is a concept, or a moral motive.
Principal means 'chief', and functions as a noun as well as an adjective. The *principals* of a firm might adopt a policy of equal opportunities as a matter of *principle*.

PROSCRIBE/PRESCRIBE:
Proscribe is to reject, banish.
Prescribe is to lay down, impose authoritatively.

STATIONERY/STATIONARY:
Stationery is notepaper, envelopes etc.
Stationary means unmoving, at a halt.
(An awful pun: your *stationery* could be *stationary* if your stock is at a standstill.)

Check if you are uncertain about word meanings.

```
I know that you will possibly find this solution as being
far from satisfactory. However, it does at the end of the
day give you a contractural lean over the roofer ...
                                            (Anon)
```

Anyone who persists in spelling *contractual* as 'contractural' is in for a *lien* time.

Cause and effect
'Due to' can be used in three ways.

EXAMPLES:
(a) *The employer paid the money due to the contractor*
(ie something is owed to someone).

(b) *The concert is due to start at 7 pm*
(ie something is expected to happen).

38

(c) *The bricks had cracked due to frost damage*
(ie something has been caused).

Using *due to* to indicate cause and effect (c) can lead to awkward constructions. The same applies to *owing to. Because (of)* is simpler and usually results in more fluent expression.

EXAMPLES:
(a) *I was late this morning because my train was cancelled.*
(b) *I was late this morning due to my train being cancelled.*
(c) *I was late this morning owing to the cancellation of my train.*

'Fewer than' or 'less than'?
There is a simple way to find out which you should write. *Fewer than* and *less than* answer the questions *How many?* and *How much?* respectively. Use *fewer than* for numbers of items; *less than* for measured quantities.

EXAMPLES:
(a) *In the cellar fewer than* [How many?] *six bottles of burgundy were left.*

(b) *The piggybank yielded less than* [How much?] *£20.*

'Like' or 'as'?
Both *like* and *as* are used to express similarities. The difference is that *like* is used where one thing resembles another, whereas *as* is used to compare actions and situations. *As* introduces adverbial clauses of manner or degree.

EXAMPLES:
(a) *My love is like a red, red rose.*
(b) *It's twelve miles as the crow flies.*

Feel like and *look like* have double meanings which make those who yearn for a tidy language despair. See Peregrine's personal problem in Fig 1.0:
'Most mornings, I feel like a boiled egg'.

3.5 Be consistent

This means making decisions about details. For example, how headings are to be weighted; where initial capital letters are to be used; how to describe people and organisations. The notes on preparing material for publication in Section 11 may be helpful. Decide whether to use a singular or plural verb after collective nouns, such as group, cooperative, building society, bank, design team and so on according to the meaning. The problem is that although the collective concept is singular, its constituents are obviously plural and logically require a plural verb.

EXAMPLES:

(a) *The committee is going to meet on alternate Fridays.*

(b) *The design team were delighted with the QS's report.*

Plural items following a collective noun often 'attract' a following verb into the plural:

(c) *A series of incidents have* [has] *occurred over the last six months.*

The same happens after pronouns such as *none, any, either, neither, everyone*:

(d) *None of the bricks have* [has] *cracked so far.*

Strictly speaking, all these pronouns are singular (*no one, any one, which one, either one* etc) and should take a singular verb.

The Reverend W A Spooner got it (more or less) right:

'Which of us has not felt in his heart a half-warmed fish?'

3.6 Test what you have written

Read back what you have written slowly and carefully (preferably aloud or, if that would alarm your colleagues, under your breath). If you have to re-read any part, or if you find you have to pause, something probably needs improvement or correction, or simply better punctuation. If your own writing makes you pause, it will probably bring the reader to an abrupt halt. This does not mean that we should write in the way we speak. Far from it: speech is essentially spontaneous and opportunistic – what we say evolves as we go along, and our syntax shifts and reforms accordingly – whereas writing is a controlled and deliberate form of communication.

Mark any 'halt' points as you go along and when you have read through the whole piece, go back to them. Assuming that you have got your facts right, what is amiss? It could be an ambiguity or uncertainty of meaning, an odd turn of phrase, some misplaced punctuation or an uncomfortable word order. Or is it a general lack of fluency?

Fluency and ease of comprehension can be improved if you avoid some of the pitfalls discussed in 3.7.

3.7 Pitfalls to be avoided

Passive v. active

Avoid the passive voice – use the active. Compare *The drawings were discovered by us to be inaccurate* with *We discovered that the drawings were inaccurate.*

In the past the passive has traditionally been used in scientific reporting to enhance the impression of impartial observation (*the water was observed to boil* instead of *the water was boiling*). Wherever possible use the active; the passive is stodgy, unwieldy and creates a barrier between writer and reader. It gives an impression of 'ivory tower' pontification.

Use the passive *deliberately* for emphasis.

EXAMPLES:
(a) I have lost my hat [neutral statement].
(b) *My hat has been found!* [marked statement].

Noun v. participle

Avoid *the (noun) of*; use the present participle. Compare *by means of the use of* with *by using*; *by the modification of the windows* with *by modifying the windows*, *for the selection of a contractor* with *for selecting a contractor.*

This is a common bad habit. Alter any business letter you have at hand in this way and see how its fluency improves.

Introductory v. real subject

Avoid the introductory subject; use the real subject. Compare *It was the general view that* with *The general view was that*; *There was a feeling of dissatisfaction on the part of the client* with *The client felt dissatisfied*; *It is the intention of the insurers to* with *The insurers intend to.* But use this construction deliberately for emphasis, eg 'It was the *contractor* who noticed the leak' (not the clerk of works).

41

Long v. short words

Avoid long words where shorter ones will do, such as *commence* instead of *begin, requirement* instead of *need, procure* instead of *get, consider* instead of *think, assistance* instead of *help*.

The long alternatives are mostly Latin-derived and are often chosen because they seem more 'important'. What is really important is to get your message across concisely and clearly.

Parcels of apposited nouns

Avoid groups of modifying nouns. Compare *the tenant design process participation* with *the participation of tenants in the design process*.

This growing habit reflects the influence of media journalese, eg POPE MURDER BID SUSPECT IS FREED, SOVIET RAILWAYS MINISTER'S JOB ON LINE (see 1.3). The juxtaposition of two nouns such as *icecream freezer* or *telephone table* is fine, but long strings compress rather than express what is meant, so that readers have to juggle the words to unravel the meaning. It is a weak technique, not least because the important word comes at the end of the list. In the expanded version it comes at the front.

Strings of possessives

Avoid strings of possessives. These are more common in speech: *You remember my sister's friend's cat? It's eaten next-door's little girl's budgie*. Revise a clause rather than write *the client's solicitor's objections were noted*.

'Meaningful' clichés

Avoid overworked words and phrases such as *meaningful relationship, at this point in time, charismatic, caring, to name but a few, monstrous carbuncle, quantum leap*. (Also avoid items of bureaucratic gobbledegook such as *creative delay* etc. See 'Eurospeak', 3.1.)

All these weaken what you are trying to say because whatever meaning they might have had once has been exhausted by over-use.

Flatulent modifiers

Avoid over-using modifiers such as *very, quite, somewhat, rather* etc. They make your style flabby. There is rarely any difference between *difficult* and *very difficult, sad* and *awfully sad, clear* and *absolutely clear, satisfactory* and *highly satisfactory, dry* and *really dry*. Leave them out.

Trailing prepositions

Avoid ending sentences with prepositions, such as *This is not the survey that the contractor referred to,* instead of *This is not the survey to which the contractor referred.*

A well-constructed sentence is enhanced by ending with a bit of weight. A plump, polysyllabic noun has more impact than a trailing preposition. However, some sentences that end with a preposition cannot be 'corrected' simply by shifting the preposition to the start of the clause. There are many verbs whose meaning changes or is modified by a following preposition, so that it can't be detached.

EXAMPLES:
(a) *I didn't understand what he was getting at.*
(b) *Removing old wallpaper is something that I usually try to get out of.*
(c) *That is something I will not put up with!*

You will have noticed that the verbs in question are typically semi-colloquial; there are more formal alternatives. *Meant* would do for example (a); and *endure* or *tolerate* would suit example (c). Example (b) is more of a problem, as the semantics are not easy to match. (*You get on with it, dear, as you're so good at it, while I nip down to the chippy . . .*) The flavour of sweet-talk and a swift exit can't be conveyed by *miss* or *forgo.* Tricky situations of this kind are sometimes resolved by a quiet moment with *Roget's Thesaurus.*

Dangling participles
Present participles (ie verbs + *ing* such as *singing, writing, lifting*) have to be attached to a noun or pronoun to avoid confusion.

EXAMPLES:
(a) *He walked away, swinging his stick jauntily.*
(b) *Laughing, she picked up the umbrella.*
(c) *Jill ran home crying her eyes out.*

Now consider the sentence in Fig 1.0:
'Lifting the floorboards, dry rot was apparent.'

Lifting is unattached to anyone or anything. The sentence should have run something like:
On lifting the floorboards, I noticed some dry rot.

But don't confuse this construction with present participles used as part of a noun *phrase* (enclosed in brackets in the next examples).

EXAMPLES:

(a) *(Writing good English) is not easy.*

(b) *One of my favourite activities is (riding a bicycle).*

(c) *(Having a good time) was all that they cared about.*

Noun phrases sometimes become awkward in use, typically where they are 'possessed' by a noun or pronoun. It is often better to rephrase.

EXAMPLE:

(a) *Your losing your temper at that moment only made matters worse.*

In speech, this would probably be uttered as *You losing your temper* . . . . You can see why: possessive noun/pronoun + noun phrase is an uncomfortable construction. Prefer

(b) *By losing your temper at that moment, you only made matters worse.*

Similarly,

(c) *Jane's always being polite to clients has not gone unnoticed*

is much better expressed as

(d) *It has not gone unnoticed that Jane is always polite to clients.*

Hanging clauses

'Built in 1932, Hoopers Park is a pseudo-Tudor development of 24 detached houses arranged around a central
courtyard.'

The sentence begins with an introductory adjectival clause *Built in 1932* . . .. Avoid 'hanging' clauses such as this; they delay the arrival of the subject so that the reader is kept waiting for enlightenment, and fluency of communication vanishes. This construction is much loved by journalists and writers of blurbs of all kinds. Businesslike it is not.

Feeling clients . . .

Keep personification out of business correspondence, even though it manifests itself constantly in the media, eg

This week sees the end of the football season.
The whole stadium leapt to its feet.

Avoid, for example

This report views the matter with concern.
The plant installation pleads for a more generous budget.
The area cries out for conservation.

44

And, another common habit, don't use *feel* when you mean *think* or *consider*, eg

The client feels the tender figure is too high.
We feel we cannot comment at this stage.

... and bored contractors?

Commuters approaching Kings Cross on the Midland City line must often spare a sympathetic thought for the diminutive, yawn-stifling Murphys:

> J. & M. MURPHY
> Short bored piling contractors

Section 4

Signals and devices

4.1 Emphasis

In writing we can use simple visual signals to help compensate for all the ways we make speech interesting and compelling, such as gestures, facial expressions and body language generally.

Without such assistance, communication of any kind would be boring and much of it would be pointless. Without any means of emphasis, we have deadpan statements.

EXAMPLES:
(a) *John ate the apple*

With emphasis, we have
(b) John *ate the apple*/John ate the *apple*, or
(c) It was John *who ate the apple*/It was the apple *that John ate*

In typescript, you underline when you want to turn a neutral, unmarked sentence into a marked one to reflect your evaluation of what you are communicating. In published material, the underlined words usually become italicised. However, there are also many grammatical and syntactical devices for achieving thematic focus and impact. We have already discussed the special roles of *and* and *but* in this respect (see 2.4), and also the special use of the passive voice (see 3.7). If you are interested in pursuing the matter further, refer to Appendix 1.

Writers use emphasis to reflect their subjective view and interpretation of events. The more subjective they become, the livelier and more informal their style of writing becomes.

4.2 Quotation marks and apostrophes

QUOTATION MARKS
Apart from their function in defining quotations, they are used to indicate that words are being used to convey some other meaning

with which the writer does not necessarily agree. For instance, someone might refer to 'bad' grammar thus, because although they might not support the view that grammar can be bad, they acknowledge that others do.

APOSTROPHES

Apostrophes have two main functions. They can
- indicate an abbreviation (a, b)
- indicate possession (c, d)

EXAMPLES:
(a) *It's* [it is] *time for tea.*
(b) *John's* [John is] *coming today.*
(c) *John's friend* [the friend of John] *is coming to tea.*
(d) *The hat's feather* [the feather of the hat] is missing.

The function of the apostrophe to mark an abbreviation (as in *it's, don't, haven't* etc) is clear enough. However, its use as an indicator of possession often causes some confusion.

The possessive (genitive) case is indicated by
('s), eg *John's hat, Mary's mother,* or

(') after a noun ending in *s,* eg *Ray Jones' dog, the Joneses' cat* (the plural of Jones is Joneses).

This is all straightforward until you encounter possessive pronouns, which are irregular. (When items are described as 'irregular', it usually means that no one has been able to come up with a logical explanation for them.)

I, you, he/she, it, we, they become
My, your, his/her, its, our, their.

Note that the possessive of *it* is *its* — no apostrophe. This distinguishes it from *it's* meaning *it is.* Now consider the next examples.

EXAMPLES:
(a) *Whose hat is this?*
   It's mine/yours/his/hers/ours/theirs (no apostrophes)

but

(b) *It's John's, Mary's, my auntie's, Sarah Jones'* etc, and in

(c) *I never liked that dog* of theirs/*husband* of hers
there seems to be *double* possession!

4.3 Brackets and dashes

Square brackets have various special editorial functions (for example,
in some of the grammatical examples in this book), and their use should
be avoided in non-technical material. Round brackets (*parentheses*) are
used to enclose 'asides' or informational remarks. So are double dashes
and so are pairs of commas. All these indicate the interesting linguistic
device known as *interpolation*, which is a means of bringing the sentence
to a halt so as to throw in some observation, or to mitigate what has
gone before, or to add something. *Interpolation* is discussed more fully
in Appendix 1.

4.4 Listing

In running text, don't list more than seven items. Research has
shown that seven is the maximum number that can be mentally
digested by the receiver. This advice is heeded in this programme
write-up in *Radio Times*.

'High above the earth's surface, David Attenborough floats weightless,
showing that without gravity the world would be a chaotic place. Seeds,
spiders, sky-diving frogs, gliding squirrels, insects, birds and bats have
all overcome the force of gravity to fly through the air.'

Use bullet points for long lists of short items such as a checklist.
Use (a), (b), (c) for setting out alternatives. Semi-colons can be used
to separate them. Number lists of points where you and the recipient
need them for reference (eg, *I have asked the quantity surveyor to comment
on point (3) in your letter*).
   Any kind of listing
● helps to break up the text, and
● draws attention to the items being discussed.

4.5 Sequence

Sequence is important in syntax (ie in putting words together to make a sentence) as well as in developing a theme. If you get it wrong, your description or argument won't hang together. It is a matter of logic as much as chronology. Some years ago the *Harpenden Weekly News* used one of the following slogans to advertise itself. Which, do you think?

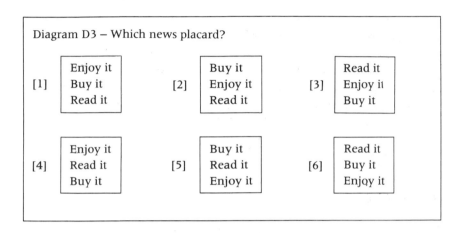

Diagram D3 – Which news placard?

[1] Enjoy it / Buy it / Read it

[2] Buy it / Enjoy it / Read it

[3] Read it / Enjoy it / Buy it

[4] Enjoy it / Read it / Buy it

[5] Buy it / Read it / Enjoy it

[6] Read it / Buy it / Enjoy it

(5) is the right answer, of course. Whenever you have a series of points to make or items to list, check that they are sensibly arranged within themselves as well as in a logical order appropriate to your theme.

It is important to get word order right to avoid confusion and ambiguity. A comfortable arrangement of words enhances fluency.

EXAMPLES:

(a) *I, to get a second opinion, will, on Friday, telephone Counsel.*

(b) *The two houses, completed recently in Cranmere Gardens, are for sale now.*

(c) *On TV, somebody said last night that the end, as we know it, of civilisation is approaching.*

A proliferation of commas is needed to compensate for the awkward word order. The unscrambled versions don't need any:

(d) *I will telephone Counsel on Friday to get a second opinion.*

(e) *The two houses recently completed in Cranmere Gardens are now for sale.*

(f) *Last night on TV someone said that the end of civilisation as we know it is approaching.*

49

Most of us instinctively know how to order a long string of words that modify the meaning of a noun. Try the following examples.

EXAMPLES:
(g) *Hats old rather five tin shabby Peter's*
(h) *Dresses smocked green two nicely linen those summer very*

Not difficult, but was it instinctive? Or did you *know* that there was an invariable order for most of the items?

There are four categories of premodifying words in examples (g) and (h):

1   Determiners [which one(s)?], eg *those, all the, Cecilia's*
2   Enumerators [how many?], eg *one, ten, a million, numerous*
3   Adverbs of manner/degree [how/to what extent?], eg *quite, extremely, neatly, cautiously*
4   Adjectives [describe/define], eg *red, tight, dark, amiable*
5   Apposited nouns [function as adjs], eg *tin, summer*, in D4

Diagram D4 – Sorting out word order

1 DET	2 EN	3 ADV	4 ADJ	5 NOUN
Peter's	*five*	*rather*	*1 shabby* *2 old*	*1 tin* *2 hats*
Those	*two*	*1 very* *2 nicely*	*1 smocked* *2 green* *3 linen*	*1 summer* *2 dresses*

Parsing is *such* sweet sorrow.

Part 2

Writing in practice

Section 5

Writing letters

I enclose a copy of an Architect's Instruction which
covers an additional manhole which was not known about as
it was beneath the earth's surface but was discovered by
our Mr Brown under the porch slab.

(Anon)

Writing a letter is not the only way to respond to a request, written or otherwise, or to obtain information. Alternatives are the telephone, telex, and fax. There may be occasions when nothing less than a personal visit can resolve a situation.

You should write a letter if you need to record some action taken, request made or information given. A letter exists on paper, whereas a phone call vanishes without trace unless the caller or recipient makes a record of it. It can be corrected or revised, copied to others and eventually filed away for future reference. Of course, it is slower to arrive than a phone call (assuming that the person in question is available to take the call) and it is often forgotten that letters are expensive. Quite apart from postal charges, they require thinking time, drafting or dictation time, typing time, copying time and filing time. And time costs money.

Phone calls are best for transmitting simple information and getting immediate feedback, making appointments, arranging meetings and getting quick results in urgent situations. But remember that anything important will have to be followed up by a letter anyway. If you need someone's written agreement urgently, you could enclose a photocopy of your letter for signature and immediate return.

Phone calls are also useful for sounding out opinions confidentially when you don't want to commit yourself to paper – they can be 'off the record'. Sometimes you may want them to be 'on the record'. If so, you must write up a file note as soon as you ring off, and sign and date it. Always have a memo pad near your telephone for making notes during phone calls, and head them with the name of the caller and the date (see Fig 8.0, which shows example headings). Do the same if people drop in to see you. It may seem delightfully casual, but there's usually a reason for it.

Figure 5.0 sums up the writing versus speaking advantages and disadvantages. Whatever the situation, speaking is essentially informal,

53

transient and spontaneous; writing is formal, permanent and must be crafted.

FIG 5.0
Writing versus speaking

WRITING   Is best for non-urgent, complicated subject matter
Is a permanent record
Can be corrected, revised
Can be copied
Is time-consuming to produce
Is formal, structured and crafted
Is explicit, non-repetitive
Is good for transmitting complex information, or where a
detailed reply is needed

But: *Is expensive*
Recipient may not reply for a long time, requiring follow-up letters and calls

SPEAKING   Is best for urgent matters
Is immediate
Can be used for off the record probing
Is good for transmitting simple information and getting results quickly
Is cheap if kept brief and to the point

But: *Vanishes unless you make a note and copy it*
May have to be confirmed in writing
Recipient may not be immediately available
May be expensive if long distance, or at peak time, or if you or recipient ramble on

---

Once you have decided that you need to write a letter, you must decide *how* you are going to write it. This will depend on what kind of logistical help is to hand, which in turn will depend upon the stage your career has reached. It will also be influenced by current administrative and secretarial procedures, and these may be described in the office manual (see 8.7). If you are setting up in practice, then you will develop your own in response to events and maintain or discard them with experience.

5.1 Composing letters

Fig 5.1 demonstrates a systematic approach. The conventional wisdom that letters require a beginning, a middle and an end is often ignored, but it is based on sound commonsense. Each element has a distinct and proper function.

FIG 5.1   Date
The shape of a letter

Your ref
Our ref (*may include project number*)

(*Name*)
(*Address*)

Dear . . .

(*Name of project*)

(*Beginning of letter*)
Thank for letter of (date)
State context of request

(*Middle of letter*)
Reply as requested, or
Make request for information, state action required

(*End of letter*)
Sum up
Restate view, request
Final greeting

Yours . . .

(*Your name*)
Encs (or Atts) . . .

Copies to: . . .

BEGINNING

The first paragraph is always a 'scene setter'. If the letter being written is a response, then it 'thanks' (the polite way of acknowledgment) the sender, and mentions the date of the letter received (to identify it). If it is initiating correspondence it should act out its purpose, the three most common being a request, an instruction, or a review of progress.

You cannot write to a client: *Dear Mr and Mrs Goldfinch, You are asking for trouble by insisting on using a non-standard form of contract.* Not if you want to keep the Goldfinches as your clients and build up a valuable professional relationship with them. You must do a little ground work by establishing the context of your request or enquiry. It is sensible as well as elegant to lead your readers up to the matter in question; do it well and you will predispose them to agreeing with you or acceding to your request.

EXAMPLE:
Dear Mr and Mrs Goldfinch,
'Treetops', Blackheath Road
You will recall that at our meeting last week we discussed what form of contract would be appropriate for the 'Treetops' project. Because of your misgivings about . . . you said you intended to use the non-standard form suggested by the contractor.

Whilst I share your concern that . . . I can assure you that Clause . . . of IFC 84, the JCT intermediate standard form of building contract deals with such a contingency. As I mentioned to you last week, there are a number of risks attached to using a non-standard form. One is that . . . . And so on.

MIDDLE

The middle part of the letter will vary in length, depending on the subject being tackled. It is important that the letter is not too long overall. Letters of more than two pages of single-spaced typescript tend to give the recipient a sinking feeling. If you need to write at length, then consider putting the information into notes with a brief covering letter. This will result in a welcome change of form between the two elements (notepaper and report paper), a change of format and a change of writing style (letter style and notes style). If appropriate, you could add a diagram or sketch or newspaper cutting. All these can help to make lengthy communication more interesting and digestible.

Where your purpose is to update the addressee about progress made, the alternative is to write a short report under a brief covering letter. The important thing here is to remember that any action required as a result of the report must be repeated in the letter, as must any other matter to which you want to draw attention (see 7.1).

END
However long or short the middle part of a letter, the end element has a separate function. Here the object is to sum up, re-state any actions required and make a graceful and appropriate exit. This gives you the valuable opportunity to repeat, briefly and perhaps more cogently, what you have already said or requested.

The 'graceful exit' is the counterpart of the gentle lead-in in the opening paragraph. Final greetings remind the reader of the pleasant aspects of professional relationships – even though the body of your letter may have been complaining about precisely the opposite!

Getting the tone right

Your judgment of the recipient and your awareness of the situation between you will decide the tone of your letter. However skilful you are or become at the mechanics of letter-writing, there are some areas which you must tread with extra caution.

HUMOUR
A sense of humour is a prized human attribute, something that we know *we* have in abundance and which we look for in our spouses, colleagues and secretaries. However, it is strictly individualistic and therefore a 'variable'. Don't risk it in business correspondence unless you are one hundred percent sure of your ground; it could as easily hit the wrong note as the right.

FLATTERY
Another danger area. To succeed, flattery must be so subtle as to be imperceptible. It is really a form of insincerity even when it is completely well-intentioned. If it is seen through, you will feel foolish and the recipient will wonder what you *really* think of him or her.

SYMPATHY
You personally or you representing your practice will at some time have to write a letter of condolence. Even the most accomplished writers find this difficult. Too often we are the victims of our own diffidence, afraid of offending or hurting someone already in distress.

In spite of this, remember that letters of condolence *do* comfort the bereaved by their very existence as tangible evidence of the affection and esteem in which the deceased person was held. They are usually carefully kept and re-read many times.

So write with gentleness and sincerity in ordinary everyday language; don't resort to embarrassing euphemisms and platitudes such as *passing over, loved one, sad demise* and *the hereafter*. Always offer something: sympathy, practical help, prayers. Don't worry about writing a letter of great linguistic beauty; what the recipient needs is a letter that is written from the heart.

TACT

Dear Norman
Site meeting No 12: 14 July 1988
*Thank you for the draft minutes. I have suggested (marked on
the copy attached) two or three minor amendments.*

*Item 4(b) about replacing the flashings at Bowers gave us pause
for thought, as neither Bill nor I can remember recommending that
'PG Tips would be preferable subject to their performance in windy
conditions'. We suspect that something from your Catering Committee
meeting has sneaked in. Word processing is full of surprises!* Perhaps
you would kindly amend with the solution agreed under Item 4(a).
Yours sincerely*

Let your friends and colleagues (and, to be magnanimous, even your enemies) down lightly and they may do the same for you.

GETTING TOUGH

Unfortunately, real-life business problems cannot always be solved by a civilised exchange of correspondence, and it is sometimes essential to take a tough line.

However great the temptation, don't trap someone in a corner with no way out. Always leave room to manoeuvre (that includes you). If the other person is going to have to 'climb down', allow him or her to do so without losing face. Total humiliation is not the answer if you want the business relationship to continue after this particular dispute is over.

*It can happen, by the way, when 'deleted' material stored temporarily in the wp's memory is spewed up by mistake.

For settling those minor, but irritating, outstanding matters or payments which are part and parcel of running a business, it is a good idea to have a standard procedure for issuing reminder letters, such as the set of examples below.

LETTER ONE:
(Heading)
We do not seem to have received a reply to our letter of (date) about this matter/enclosing our invoice etc. Would you please confirm that you have received it and that you are giving it your attention?

LETTER TWO:
(Heading)
We refer to our letters of (date) and (date). Would you please let us have your reply by the (date)/end of the week?

LETTER THREE:
(Heading)
We are sorry to note that you have not replied to our letters of (date), (date) and (date). In such circumstances, our standard practice is to withdraw service/credit/instruct solicitor etc. We are reluctant to do so in your case, and hope that your immediate response will make such action unnecessary.

Then give them a few days' grace. Then take the action you have threatened. Never threaten unless you mean it. Once the word gets round, you won't have to do it often.

Layout and presentation

It may be stating the obvious, but letters must be dated correctly and include references (yours and theirs) and the name and full address of the person to whom you are writing. Address the recipient of your letter *Ms/Mr J Bloggs or J Bloggs Esq.* (Americans prefer the *Ms/Mr* form.) *Esq* is more usual if you have met J Bloggs. You would begin both letters *Dear Ms/Mr Bloggs* or *Dear Jane/Jack* and end *Yours sincerely.* Strictly formal letters, such as one to *The County Architect*, would begin *Dear Sir/Madam* and end *Yours faithfully.* Make sure you don't confuse the formal and informal modes and produce a hybrid such as *Dear Sir — Yours sincerely.*

Above all, make sure that the addressee's name is correctly spelt and that you have got their title right. This is fundamental; many people are profoundly irritated if they are incorrectly addressed. For example (and in the spirit of Lady Bracknell), to address someone once as *Mr* instead of *Ms/Mrs* might simply indicate carelessness; to persist in so doing might seem to imply some criticism! If in doubt, ring up the addressee's office and ask, or consult the relevant directory.

All letters should have their subject headings typed in capital letters, or bold or underlined. This helps to identify, file and retrieve them easily. The heading may include a job number, or this may be part of the letter reference. Don't use *Re:* before the heading: it's old-fashioned and unnecessary.

The preferred modern style of layout is 'blocked' to the left of the page, ie there are no indented paragraphs. (The French refer to this as *la méthode américaine*, and still prefer the indented *méthode française*, see Appendix 2.) Punctuation is not included in dates and addresses. Figs 8.6 and 8.7 are typed examples of the blocked layout.

Don't forget to check your letter through again after typing, and make sure that all enclosures or attachments have been prepared for posting and appropriate copies made and marked up. Attach a compliments slip to any carbon copies, because these may not show your office address and other details. Write or type on the slip the name of the addressee, or it may go astray at the receiving end.

Never use a compliments slip instead of a letter where transmittal needs to be recorded, particularly in the case of drawings. Their issue and description must be carefully recorded (and acknowledged in the best of all possible worlds) on a special Register of Drawings Issued form. (Refer to the *Architect's Job Book*).

You may sometimes want to copy some item for information to someone whose name is not included in the circulation list, but you may not want the person to whom the letter is addressed to see that you have done so. In that case, send a 'blind' (unmarked) copy, probably with a note of explanation.

Remember to sign the letter and initial all the copies, including the file copy. This is always advisable with formal correspondence and is a good habit to cultivate. Unless your name and status appear on the firm's headed notepaper (which is usual in the case of directors, partners and associates) the name of the firm should be typed under your signature, thus:

> (Gloria Transit)
> *Office Manager*
> *for Sparrow and Grebe*

Always read through the completed letter as if you were standing in the shoes of the recipient. Ask yourself whether, on first reading, you would perceive immediately how to respond. A letter that leaves the recipient in any doubt has failed.

FIG 5.2
Checklist for letter

1   *Does it include*
    correct title, name, address of recipient
    references, theirs and yours
    job number, date?

2   *Is the mode correct*
    formal/informal?

3   *Have I referred correctly to their letter*
    date, heading?

4   *Have I fully understood what it says?*

    Have I said what I wanted to say clearly, concisely and appropriately?

    Will they know
    what I am talking about?
    what they have to do now?
    whether I expect a response and, if so, when?

5   *Should I remind or reassure them about anything before I sign off?*

    Is the final greeting correct and appropriate?

    Have the proper enclosures been added?

    Has the letter been copied
    to the right people?
    at the right address?

6   *Has the letter been properly laid out?*
    Is it pleasing to look at?
    Has the spelling been checked?
    Are typing corrections unobtrusive?

7   *Is the file copy exactly the same as the despatched version?*

8   *Have I signed the letter and initialled the copies?*

The checklist Fig 5.2 has reminders which both you and your secretary may find helpful. If you establish this kind of critical routine in your early days in business, it will become a built-in part of your approach to letter writing.

5.2 Techniques for drafting and dictation

Letters can be drafted by hand, dictated to someone or into a recording machine, or typed straight on to a word processor. There are pitfalls to be avoided with each of these techniques and you will come to prefer or detest one or other after much trial and error. Some types of writing are better suited to one technique than another.

Drafting letters by hand

Remember that someone else is going to have to decipher your handwriting. Terrible writing is not a sign of lovable idiosyncrasy; it is time-wasting and self-indulgent. The secretary will have to refer your draft back to you (more than once, maybe). You will have to stop what you are doing to decipher it. You may, unjustly, feel irritated; the secretary may, justly, feel hard done by and consign your draft to the bottom of the typing heap or, bristling, type it and make stressful mistakes. Which is even more annoying . . . and so on.

So take a little time and care. Use lined A4 paper, such as a scribbler pad, or make up a form (Fig 5.3), taking advice from the secretarial staff, if you are wise. Use a pen with a fine fibre tip or similar, as most secretaries complain about biro-handwritten drafts and object strongly to anything written in pencil. Mark inserts and deletions clearly and write out difficult names, unusual words and technical terms in capital letters. Take special care to make numbers and quantities legible. Allow yourself plenty of room to make revisions and corrections.

PERSONAL NOTES

Some letters must be written by hand for the sake of politeness. You may dismiss this as mere etiquette, but the fact is that you may offend someone by ignoring what they may consider a 'norm'. The same applies to personal notes of thanks, congratulations, condolence and so on. Going to the trouble of writing by hand shows that you care and are prepared to make a special effort.

Some people think it a nice touch to write in *Dear Cecilia* by hand and also the final greeting (*Yours ever, Peregrine* etc) in ordinary typed

FIG 5.3
Format for drafting letters for typing

From: ....

Date: ....   Ref/Job No:.........

How urgent? Post today/tomorrow/when ....

Who will sign? I will/ .... will/Sign for me and send

Any special instructions:

Letter to: ....

Heading: ....

Enclosures/attachments:
....
Copies to:
....

letters to close business associates. They like to go to a little extra trouble to 'personalise' their correspondence.

Dictating to a shorthand writer

It may be some time before you have or share a secretary who is able (and willing) to take shorthand dictation. You may not like the technique anyway and prefer to draft your letters by hand, but it is useful to be able to dictate competently both to people and machines, and if you sprain your writing wrist playing squash to free you from the stresses at work, there may be no alternative.

'Dictation' may conjure up a picture of a high-flying executive effortlessly uttering crisp sentences at a secretary with ineffable grooming and a slightly bored expression. This is almost certainly not you. Dictation is difficult; it needs practice and discipline. It *can* save time.

The drill is this. Read your post and decide which letters need a prompt reply and are suitable for dictation. These will generally be the uncomplicated ones. You *can* dictate drafts of more complex subject matter, but it is more sensible in that case to dictate them into a recording machine rather than to a shorthand writer, whose eyes will glaze over as you pause to rack your brains, find relevant papers, make a vital phone call and so on.

Before you start, make sure that you know what you want to say and have a clear picture of the structure of your reply. Jot down the crucial points you want to make in a logical sequence. You could make up a special form as a dictation aid and also use it for notes to accompany dictated tapes (Fig 5.4). Remember the importance of items having a beginning, a middle and an end.

The dictation session should finish by lunchtime so that the results can be typed up in the afternoon to catch the evening post. Try to fend off telephone calls and other interruptions during the dictation period so that your thoughts remain collected and coherent. It saves time in the long run.

The temptation is always to dictate more rather than less. Once you get going, the sound of your own voice becomes *quite* pleasant, and the freedom from machines and pens and pencils is *so* exhilarating, and the feeling of *power* in having someone sitting there hanging on your every word (tethered and helpless, poor thing, while you ramble on), and — Good heavens! Is it twelve o'clock already? Yes, dictation requires discipline.

It is a waste of time to dictate straightforward letters that can

FIG 5.4
Format for notes to accompany dictation

DICTATION NOTES
to accompany dictation session/tape attached

From: .... Date: .... Job No: .....

List of items dictated

1 .... 2 ....

3 .... 4 ....

5 .... 6 ....

Item 1: (notes, spellings etc)

(Add any special instructions.)

Item 2:

Item 3:

Item 4:

----

be answered or drafted by the secretary if you instruct him or her properly. And don't waste time dictating the obvious. Hand over all the relevant letters, documents and files at the end of the dictation session. An efficient secretary will add the correct titles, addresses and references, and file away the letters and replies or keep them 'pending' as appropriate.

Begin by explaining what you are going to dictate:

This is a letter to Jake Partridge of British Rail. Head it 'Underpass for wildlife at Chorley Goods Depot'. Dear Jake . . .

When you are dictating, speak clearly and not too fast. A very good shorthand writer can cope with 120 words per minute and sometimes more. Novice secretaries start at about 80 wpm. In the old days, Hansard shorthand writers used to have to be able to write at more than 200. A standard BBC news bulletin is read steadily at about 180 wpm, which should give you some idea about relative speeds.

And do try to stay put at your desk when dictating. It may seem wonderfully dynamic to stride up and down, pausing dramatically to gaze out of the window at the old gasworks, but for the shorthand writer, head well down over notebook, your voice will come and go and your gasworks-inspired observations (made with your back to him or her) will probably be totally inaudible.

Using a dictation machine

Dictation machines can be efficient and time-saving, provided your technique is good. As usual, practice makes perfect. The advantages are that you can dictate during odd gaps in the working day, stop and start as you please, and even take the machine home or away with you on site visits. Tapes can be posted back to the office for transcribing if necessary.

When you acquire a dictating machine, the first thing to do is to find out how it works and then experiment. If you have never heard it before, the sound of your recorded voice will probably make you flinch and take a vow then and there to speak more clearly. Now you know what the secretary has to put up with*.

When you dictate into a machine you have to enunciate much more deliberately than when dictating to a shorthand writer. Remember that you probably won't be around to answer questions when your tape is being transcribed. A great entertainment in secretarial offices is to see

*Try moving that trailing preposition to somewhere else in the sentence . . .

half the technical staff huddled around an audio-typist trying to make out what the Beloved Leader has committed to tape on site, apparently poised on a parapet 200 feet up in a force 8 gale.

The same advice about getting your thoughts organized before you utter them holds good. However, using a machine does allow you to switch off and think for a while, so that this technique is well suited to drafting purposes. What it does *not* allow you to do is go back to page four and insert a new paragraph. You can dictate an insert and instruct the transcriber where to include it, but your instructions must be handwritten out on a sheet of paper so that the typist sees them *before* starting on the draft (although this is no problem if a word processor is being used).

In any case, it is always a good idea to write some notes to accompany the tape to be transcribed (Fig 5.4). These should list the items on the tape and add any information which the transcriber will need to complete them. They should also include spellings of unusual words and names of places and people. Spelling out while you are dictating is often a problem. A rapid audio-typist will often have typed the word (inspirationally) before you have started to spell it out. Then he or she hears the spelling, curses, and has to amend or delete. If possible, agree in advance some special signal that the typist will recognise.

Probably the most difficult part is mastering the 'off' switch so that the end result is a fluently dictated letter. The trick is to speak at an even pace and switch off immediately you have to stop for any reason. Don't leave the machine running while you collect your thoughts, or there will be large gaps which will bring the transcriber to a halt. If possible, dictate in logical chunks with break points coinciding with punctuation (see Fig 5.5). Don't dictate in a monotone; it helps the transcriber to follow what you are saying if your intonation reflects the ups and downs of normal speech.

You can dictate faster to a machine than to a shorthand writer because audio typists are able to stop and start the tape by means of a foot pedal and catch up, or re-run parts they mishear. But it is a great help if the finished tape is fluent and free from 'thinking' gaps.

Again, don't forget to announce each item.

This is a draft report to Robin Redford, Bursar at Chorley Manor School. Title is 'Remedial work to gymnasium roof'. Double spacing, please.

Remember to add instructions about whether or not the transcribed item can be sent off in your absence. If it can, the secretary will add

FIG 5.5
How to chunk dictation

```
'Hullo Jenny/letter to Robin Redford please/the address
is in the file/

Job number 1066/today's date/Dear Jake/heading/

Chorley Manor School (colon)/New swimming pool/

Thank you for your letter of twelfth January (full
stop/new paragraph)/

We are delighted to hear/that the new swimming pool/is
to be opened on 15 May/by Sir George Winterbotham
spelt/W-I-N-T-E-R-B-O-T-H-A-M (full stop)/The
contractor foresees no difficulty/in having the pool
operational/by the end of April/provided that the
order/for the special non-slip tiles/is placed this
week with Skiptrip spelt/S-K-I-P-T-R-I-P/Products
Limited (full stop/new paragraph)/

We hope that the services consultant/will be able to
attend the next site meeting/(bracket)/third
February/(close bracket full stop)/His name is Mark
Strudel spelt/S-T-R-U-D-E-L/(full stop)/I enclose a
copy of my letter to him/(full stop new paragraph)/

Yours sincerely/'


'Jenny/please sign and send this off for me/thanks/

... Oh/don't forget to attach the copy letter/cheers/'
```

a note saying *Dictated by (name) and signed in his/her absence by (name), secretary.*

Play back each item after dictating it, and check the notes for the audio typist. When you have completed all the dictation, make a list of items dictated, wind back the tape, put it into a tape case and attach it to the list of items and any related notes before giving it to the typist.

5.3 Replying to letters

Sorting out the post is an important and often horrendous task.

Professional people get inundated with letters and literature of all kinds, much of it speculative. If you delegate the task of opening and distributing the post, make sure that it is to someone capable of recognising and discarding the rubbish. If you deal with the post yourself, identify the important letters and don't be sidetracked by the irrelevant.

As soon as a letter arrives on your desk, whether addressed to you or marked for you to deal with, read it, initial it and date it. Decide whether it can be filed or whether immediate action is needed. If neither, then keep it pending.

Respond politely

When replying to letters, the first rule is: always respond politely, even when you profoundly suspect that the writer intends to be rude, or is 'fishing', or trying to persuade you to do something that you have no intention of doing. At the seminar to launch the *Starting up in Practice* booklet, David Rock said: 'Always be nice to people!', and Oliver Willmore added: 'Never close a door behind you!'.

Don't write 'put down' one-liners, however great the temptation. Why make enemies? People who write *you* patently rude letters are trying to needle you and if you respond furiously they're winning. A bland reply will deflate them completely. Similarly, a fishing letter is best dealt with by a little exposure, such as: *I suspect that what you are really asking me is . . . and, if so, I'm afraid that I can't help you . . . .* If you are refusing something offered, or someone is trying to bludgeon you into agreement, be firm and unequivocal in saying no, otherwise a long and pointless correspondence may ensue.

Respond promptly

The second and more difficult rule is: always respond promptly. If you are being offered some opportunity, thank the writer immediately and say that you will reply fully in a few days' time. In this way you keep a foot in the door while you check out the proposition.

It is not a good idea to use ready-printed acknowledgment postcards. They give an impression of remoteness, tend to get lost or ignored and are awkward to file. There is also a danger that they may be taken as a sign that you agree with the letter received.

Ask your secretary, if you have one, to acknowledge letters appropriately on your behalf and to remind you to answer them fully in due course. If you have no secretary but do have a word processor, prepare and store a simple acknowledgment format and fill in the details as appropriate. But respond in some way immediately. If you can get into the habit of at least acknowledging letters the day they are received, you will impress your business contacts no end.

Replying to invitations
Formal invitations require a formal reply. Your reply should

- thank the person(s) issuing the invitation
- identify the event
- say whether or not you can attend.

If you can't attend, you don't have to say why (although you may like to mention it when you next see the person who has issued the invitation); simply express your regrets. Don't say you are unable to attend *because of a prior engagement*. This sounds stuffy and may indicate that you *prefer* the other event. And you need not refer to their invitation as *kind*.

Here is a typical formal reply. Type it on headed notepaper and centre the text.

EXAMPLE:

Peregrine Sparrow thanks the Directors of the ABC Development Company for their invitation to a cocktail party on 27 May 1987.

He has pleasure in accepting it

or
He regrets that he is unable to accept it.

YES, MINISTER!
Personal invitations from VIPs (we all have VIPs in our lives and they are not necessarily at ministerial level) should be be answered the day they are received in your own handwriting – formally, if the invitation is formal, otherwise a short letter. Printed invitations from personal friends can be accepted formally, but if you have to refuse then write a brief note by hand saying:

Sorry, Cecilia, no escape from mother-in-law's Pig Fancier of the Year presentation dinner that evening. Have a great party — Peregrine.

Or words to that effect.

5.4 Contract administration

```
Your sub-contract is causing very serious delays to the
Contract which as you know is being lived in by our
valued Clients.
```
                                        (Anon)

This subject is extensively covered in the 1988 edition of the *Architect's Job Book*. The example correspondence included covers letters of agreement with the client, letters of appointment, letters placing advance orders, invitations to tender and their acceptance or refusal. When the contract works are under way, there are many example letters relating to specific contract conditions, together with the relevant Architect's Instructions to put them into effect. There is also a range of specimen letters of determination of employment connected with various causal events. But first a word of warning.

Never use 'example' or 'typical' letters, wherever they are given, without properly assessing the particular situation in question. The *context* is all-important. However busy you are, never photocopy an example letter, fill in the project details and send it out. Examples are there to help you to see how facts should be marshalled and presented and what style, approach and attention to detail is needed. Typical letters can be a useful aid to the process of solving a problem; they are not solutions in themselves.

Letters, AIs, site meeting minutes and notes of inspections etc associated with contract works are part of the story of that contract and, if there is any subsequent investigation connected with litigation, they will be part of the evidence. Therefore it is crucial that they are clearly expressed and unambiguous. Many disputes arise simply because letters and instructions are misunderstood. Here are some points to remember.

Use a formal style
Letters connected with contractual matters are always formal. Start and end them *Dear Sir — Yours faithfully*. Be sure to refer to yourself as *we*, not *I*.

Get the references right
The main heading will be the name of the contract works and any project number. Always date the document as the date of issue, not the date it was drafted.

State the relevant clause in the contract
Quote the clause number in the contract that relates to the subject of the letter or AI with the name of the form of contract under which the works are being carried out. (*This request is made in accordance with Clause . . . of IFC 84.*) Check that you have got it right.

Quote drawing numbers correctly
It is equally important to quote drawing numbers and their titles exactly and fully.

Refer to events precisely
State the relevant date and where necessary the location.

Keep sentences short and language simple
Contract provisions are often expressed in a convoluted way and this tends to creep into the rest of the correspondence. Write as clearly as possible.

Remember to send copies to all the relevant parties
Some architects believe in copying all job-related correspondence to the client as a matter of course. You *must* copy all contract-related correspondence to the client.

Consult your solicitor
Be sure to do this whenever a situation arises where there may be legal repercussions; he or she will advise you in the light of the particular circumstances.

Advise your insurers
Similarly, you must advise your insurers immediately of any circumstances likely to give rise to a claim. Failure to notify in good time can be a valid reason for their refusing to indemnify you.

Don't ignore claims
Respond if claims or allegations are made, but always take legal advice about the form of your reply.

'Powers' and 'duties'
Under a building contract, the architect has 'powers' and 'duties'. Make sure you know the difference between them. A power is usually expressed as *the architect may*; a duty as *the architect shall.*

'Without Prejudice'

It is a common misconception that heading a letter 'Without Prejudice' in some way protects the author from its contents. *It only does this in certain, special circumstances.* For the purposes of business correspondence, always assume that it does *not*. Again, consult your solicitor.

It is always difficult to 'stand back' and see exactly what the words you have written *mean*. *You* know what you mean, but is that what you have written? In one well-known case, an architect cheerily promised a client that he 'would do anything necessary'. Alas for him a few years later when a lawsuit came home to roost.

5.5 A letter to the Editor

You may feel impelled to take up your pen, whether in sorrow or in indignation, and write a letter for publication in the technical or national press. To be 'correct' it should be addressed to *The Editor*, and should begin *Sir*, and end *Yours etc.*. In fact, you can begin it *Dear Sir* and end it *Yours truly/faithfully*. It doesn't matter greatly, because many editors put all published letters into a standard format anyway.

The point to remember is that this is a *formal* letter. It should be typed double-spaced on one side only of one or more sheets of white A4 paper. Write a short (and polite) covering letter on your headed notepaper, so that it is clear who you and your firm are, on the lines of Fig 5.6.

FIG 5.6
A letter to the Editor

Dear Sir

I enclose for your consideration a letter in response to the article by Joseph Avocet on page 19 of the April edition of your Journal. I hope you will be able to publish it in the correspondence column next month.

Yours faithfully

Remember that the editor has absolute discretion about publishing or rejecting letters and may even change your offering if, aflame with passion, you have thrown such necessary trivia as punctuation and spelling to the winds. If extensive changes or omissions seem to be needed, the editor will probably telephone you.

Take special care to compose the letter properly and make your points clearly; many of your peers (as well as potential clients) are going to be reading this letter and making instant judgments about you and your firm. However angry or hard-done-by you may feel, keep its tone calm and reasonable. Editors love a running correspondence between overheated professionals, but the parties to it often end up looking rather silly.

5.6 1992 et tout cela

A *frisson* is likely to run round the office when a letter written in a foreign language pops up in the mail. It may invite you to take part in a competition or symposium or – who knows? – even ask you to consider joining a project to design some prestigious building in a European capital. If you are able to respond suitably and elegantly in the writer's language you are definitely winning but, as we all know, this is unlikely.

You are lucky indeed if anyone in the office has a reasonable command of French, German or Spanish and has in addition studied and mastered the niceties of business correspondence. It is even rarer for architects practising in the United Kingdom to be able to communicate technical matters without fear of misinterpretation.

The attitude of our European professional equivalents is much less laid-back than ours. They are fiercely proud of their professional standing and have a strong sense of the proprieties and formalities of business life. The French in particular seem to rejoice in an abundant flowering of formality; they end the most prosaic of letters with entreaties to accept their profound (sometimes devoted) sentiments or beseech the recipient to be kind enough to agree their distinguished salutations. This is all very discouraging for the British, whose stiffest upper lips tend to tremble at the prospect of looking an ass in front of foreigners.

Our insular forebears used to think it was tactful to ignore the fact that foreigners lacked the benefit of having a proper language like ours; one wrote to them firmly (and spoke to them loudly) in

English. Winston Churchill's well-known alternative was to take the French language by the scruff of its neck and 'speak' it with relentless atrocity.

But times and attitudes have changed, and we are all vividly aware that 1992 approaches and with it the potential of a single market of 320 million consumers and inevitably closer contacts and ties with our European neighbours, many of whom can speak and write some of one another's languages and usually some of ours as well. So being able to write an appropriate letter in French or German or Spanish may not necessarily be a crucial *business* consideration, but it could be an impressive weapon to add to your PR artillery.

If you do consider taking on some substantial project abroad, it would probably be worth your while to engage a bi- or trilingual secretary, but these persons are rare and will naturally expect to be paid more than their monolingual counterparts. It may seem simpler to hire the services of a translator, and there may be times when you have to do so anyway. However, be warned: linguists charge high rates per hour, and the more technical the work, the more time they need for translation. (Even then, you would be wise to hedge your bets and send the English version pinned to the translation.) For translations into English, agencies often have two rates: one for a quick, rough comprehension and the other for a polished version.

In Appendix 2, *Toujours la politesse*, there is some guidance about the formalities of letter-writing so dear to the hearts of the French. It is given on the assumption that the reader already has some command of French, but is at a loss when it comes to business correspondence. The advice is not exhaustive, and if you find you are still struggling, give up and write in English. We all find vastly amusing the efforts foreigners make to write and speak our language; don't forget that the reverse is just as true.

It is *always* better to write a well-constructed, appropriate and elegant letter in English than have a totally inexpert shot at communicating architectural matters in a foreign language where the consequences of misunderstanding could be dire for all concerned.

Ponder the words of Antoine de Rivarol: *'Ce qui n'est pas clair, n'est pas français.'*

Section 6

Taking and writing minutes

The Treasurer proposed a vote of thanks to Mrs Noble, who
had been a pillar of support in the church renovations
scheme for many years.

(Anon)

Little advice is ever offered about how to approach the task of
minuting, or what techniques and procedures are needed to ensure
that minutes are an accurate and valuable record of the business of a
meeting. Architects, especially in their earlier years of practice, often
have to chair meetings *and* minute them, and find this difficult and
worrying.

Fortunately, minuting is a skill that improves with practice, although
it always needs a high level of concentration. But if you can run the
meeting efficiently and confidently, taking the minutes becomes less
of a problem.

The run-of-the-mill meetings that architects have to take are usually
project-related. They may be held on site or in your own or someone
else's office.

6.1 What are 'minutes'?

Minutes are a written record of the significant items of business
transacted at a meeting. The name is derived from the Latin *minutia*
(plural *minutiae*), meaning *detail(s)*. They have a number of important
functions:

* they record why the meeting was called, what it achieved,
  and what further actions are needed;
* they provide a record by which future progress can be measured;
* they are a means of reporting to interested parties who may
  not regularly attend site meetings;
* they constitute a record which may be relied upon in any
  future dispute.

However, where a matter of special relevance or importance arises at
the meeting, particularly if it is likely to have legal implications, it is wise

to draw attention to this in a letter to those concerned rather than to rely upon the minutes alone. This may be recorded in the 'Actions' column referred to later.

6.2 Meetings

Purpose

Everyone should have a clear idea about why a meeting is being held and what it ought to achieve. Most meetings are called to review progress and to get decisions approved. In his book *The Business of Architectural Practice* (1986), Derek Sharp reckoned that an average site meeting of seven people in a provincial town within 100 miles of London cost £2,814.50. Meetings should only be held if they are really necessary.

If you are calling a meeting, make sure that the people who are attending have the appropriate authority to act in accordance with the decisions made. If this is an initial meeting and you are not sure whom to invite from an organisation, your letter of approach to them could describe the purpose of the meeting and ask for 'appropriate representation'.

An agenda

All meetings should have a proper structure and most of them will benefit from having an agenda, which should be sent out in good time before the meeting. As well as notifying the details of the event, an agenda has the great virtue of focusing the minds of those attending before they arrive, and allows them to rehearse (mentally at least) what they want to say. They are then more likely to arrive informed and informative on the day. An agenda also helps the person in the chair to control the meeting, in that it provides a framework within which to contain discussion.

Fig 6.0 is a format for a combined notification and agenda showing the basic elements for any meeting. Fig 6.1 is the specimen agenda given in Volume 1 of the *Architect's Job Book* for an initial project meeting.

Arrangements

The uninitiated might suppose that meetings are usually held in well-lit, warm, comfortable surroundings with ample chairs and a large conference table adorned with sparkling mineral water and pristine writing materials.

77

FIG 6.0
General purpose notification and agenda

NOTIFICATION OF MEETING
AND AGENDA

Name of project   Job no.

Type of meeting   Meeting no.

This meeting will be held at Sparrow & Grebe's offices at
(time) on (date). It is expected to end at (time).

There will be a (forty minute) break for lunch/A sandwich
lunch will be provided during the meeting.

Apologies, names of replacements should be notified to (name
of architect or secretary).

A G E N D A

1   Minutes of last meeting

2   Matters arising

3   (Item for discussion)

4   ditto

5   ditto, etc.

6   Any other business

7   Date of next meeting
     (if any, with details of time and place)

Distribution: (names of people or organisations
                invited/expected to attend)

Date: (agenda was issued)

In practice, many site meetings are held in dim, draughty, dirty site huts with inadequate seating and no surface on which to rest a notepad. They are frequently interrupted by urgent telephone calls and by large well-intentioned members of the labour force bearing mugs of tea which inevitably get spilt over the notes you have so painstakingly recorded.

Try to arrange reasonable facilities for meetings and ask all concerned to try to keep disturbances to a minimum. However bad the conditions, it is still up to you (by whatever means) to come away from the meeting having written down the basis for a set of useful minutes.

COMING UP FOR AIR

If you know that the meeting will be a long one, you can arrange to break for lunch or have some sent in. Breaking for lunch disrupts continuity but provides an opportunity for informal discussion. A chance to stretch legs and get a breath of fresh air often revives spirits and cools tempers. Similarly, the arrival of a 'working lunch' in the middle of a meeting may seem a distraction, but the few minutes of relaxation it brings are often much needed and can be valuable.

SITE INSPECTIONS

Site meetings are often held in conjunction with site inspections. Which event should take place first is debatable. If the inspection is first and the meeting second, all present have the opportunity to get up-to-date with developments on site and consequently go on to the meeting fully informed. On the other hand, if the meeting is first, any important site-related matters can be checked at the ensuing inspection.

On balance, it is probably better to make the inspection first, but allow enough time afterwards to check on site any points that arise from the meeting. This sequence has the advantage of permitting some informal discussion before the meeting, which helps to minimise conflict, speed discussion and, by contributing to everyone's understanding of what is going on, simplify the task of minuting.

6.3 Taking a meeting

Keeping control

It is essential to keep control of a meeting, otherwise its value may be reduced and a great deal of time wasted. And, as we have seen, time costs money.

FIG 6.1
Agenda for initial project meeting

A G E N D A
for initial project meeting

Name of project   Job no.

----

1   Introductions   Notes

       Appointments, personnel
       Roles and responsibilities
       Project description

2   Contract

       Priorities
       Handover of production information
       Commencement and completion dates
       Insurances
       Bond (if applicable)
       Standards and quality

3   Contractor's matters

       Possession
       Programme
       Site organisation, facilities and planning
       Security
       Site restrictions
       Sub-contractors and suppliers
       Statutory undertakers
       Overhead and underground services
       Temporary services
       Proposals for quality control
       Signboards

4   Clerk of works' matters

       Roles and duties
       Facilities
       Liaison
       Dayworks
                                            (continued)

Fig 6.1 *(continued)*

5   **Consultants' matters**

Structural
Mechanical
Electrical
Others

6   **Quantity surveyor's matters**

Adjustments to tender figures
Valuation procedures
Remeasurement
VAT

7   **Communications and procedures**

Information requirements
Distribution of information
Valid instructions
Lines of communication
Dealing with queries
Local authority notices

8   **Meetings**

Pattern and proceedings
Status of minutes
Distribution of minutes

9   **Any other business**

10   **Date of next meeting**

Distribution:

Date: (agenda was issued)

Confining discussion to the points at issue usually requires good humour and diplomacy. It will soon become clear who are the garrulous, the querulous (and sometimes the bibulous). You will antagonise people if you cut them off in mid-flow; try to perfect the gentle art of intervention. On some occasions it may be desirable to allow grievances to be aired (within limits) and to encourage the less articulate and self-confident to have their say. Once people realise that you are prepared to be reasonable and considerate but will not tolerate time-wasting and pointless argument, your meetings will run smoothly.

Make a point of beginning meetings on time. This will eventually discourage latecomers, whose arrival is always disruptive and who may need to be given a résumé of the proceedings so far. This is a waste of everybody's time.

Getting under way

Begin by calling the meeting to order firmly but pleasantly. Then identify those present, introduce newcomers or replacements, ask for apologies for absence and read out any that have been sent in. If appropriate, ask if everyone has received a copy of the minutes of the last meeting and, if so, whether they may be approved. Note any corrections that are suggested and *agreed*. (As a general rule, allow someone to amend the record of what *he or she* has said, not what someone else has said.) Acceptance of the previous minutes should be recorded under Item 1 of the new set of minutes (see Fig 6.2). It is wise to follow these formal procedures; if you do not, you may leave some matters open to doubt subsequently.

It is then usual to take *Matters Arising* from the previous minutes. Discussion of these may be lengthy, and there is often an attempt to introduce new topics under this item or raise items already included in the agenda. Such intrusions should be resisted; the proper place for new topics is under *Any Other Business* at the end of the meeting, whilst discussion of an agenda item should not take place until you call that item at the proper time.

It is best to run through the previous minutes heading by heading in a brisk way that indicates that you know everyone is anxious to get on to the main business of the meeting. However, you should make a note of any important points made and include them in the next set of minutes under *Matters Arising* with their previous numerical references (see Fig 6.2).

Then take the items listed on the agenda, only departing from the

FIG 6.2
Layout for minutes of a design team meeting

Name of project   Job no.

M I N U T E S
of **Design Team Meeting** no. ......
held at Sparrow and Grebe's office on ....

Present:

Apologies:

                                                        ACTION

1   **Minutes of last meeting**
    Agreed, subject to the correction of item 5(b)
    of the previous minutes:
            in line 2, delete ... and substitute ...

2   **Matters arising**
    (a) (title and reference as in previous minutes)
    (b) etc.

3   **Design team and reports**

4   **Brief**

5   **Site**

6   **Approvals**

7   **Design and cost control**

8   **Contract**

9   **Any other business**
    (a) (new items for discussion)
    (b) etc.

10 **Date of next meeting**

Distribution:

set order if there is an urgent reason for doing so. It is useful to sum up at the end of each item, especially if discussion has been lengthy, and to repeat the decisions made and actions to be taken. Allow yourself enough time to write down the minute before going on to the next item on the agenda.

When these have all been properly dealt with, ask whether there are any items to be discussed under *Any Other Business*. (Keep tight control at this point, as some burning issue which may have been simmering throughout the meeting may now explode.) Lastly, agree the date for the next meeting, if any, thank those present for attending and make sure that your notes are in order and that you have a copy of any item tabled during the meeting.

Making notes

It is unusual for architects to be able to write shorthand. In any case, it is safer to write out important notes in longhand, even if you have to halt the proceedings to do so. As well as allowing you to write a proper minute, this may remind the voluble that *you* are in control of the meeting. However, avoid breaking off for too long as people easily become restless and impatient, sub-meetings develop, there is general chat and your control begins to be undermined. The object is to get down enough notes to allow you to write up an accurate minute later; don't try to write the final version as you go along until you have become a seasoned minuter.

You may be thinking that using a recording machine at a meeting would save time, result in more accurate minutes, and spare your nerves. This is an illusion. You will have reams of material to sort through afterwards, and in any case many people dislike the idea of everything they say being recorded verbatim.

6.4 Drafting the minutes

7.   Any Other Business

   (a)   The clerk of works complained that one of the
         tenants played the flute in his pyjamas.
                                        (Anon)

It is important to draft the minutes whilst the meeting is still fresh in your mind. The layout (Fig 6.2) should follow the pattern of the agenda.

84

What to include?

The art of writing good minutes is being able to identify priorities. It is *essential* to record some things (decisions, actions to be taken) and *relevant* to record others (changes in situation, strongly opposing views). It may be *desirable* to include some parts of the remaining grey areas – and equally desirable to exclude others. This is where you must exercise your discretion. Bear in mind what has already been said about points of legal importance and make sure that you correctly link people with views expressed and actions to be taken.

An 'Actions' column

Some architects like to include an 'Actions' column down the side of the page of minutes, others to note 'Actions arising' in the text under each item. The argument against an Actions column is that readers tend to run their eye down it, pick out *their* item and ignore the rest. This may defeat the object of circulating minutes as a means of disseminating information, but at least it makes it more likely that people will take the action required and will attend the next meeting armed with the necessary information. Fig 6.2 suggests a structure for a design team meeting chaired by the architect, based on the example given in Volume 1 of the fifth edition of the *Architect's Job Book.*

6.5 The style of the minutes

Formal minutes are written in 'reported speech'. Events are put into the past, and the style is observational. This means that:

- *Pronouns have to change*
from the first or second person to the third (*I, we, you, mine, our, your* etc to *he/she, they, his/her, their* etc).

- *Tenses have to change*
from the present to the past (*say* to *said*),
from the past to the remoter past (*said* to *had said*),
from the simple future to the conditional (*will say* to *would say*).

- *Time signals have to change*
now to *then, today* to *that day, tomorrow* to *the next day, Tuesday next* to *the following Tuesday* (or insert the actual date).

Fortunately, most speakers naturally use simple tenses and the minutes should do likewise. If complexity or lack of clarity threatens as a result of translating verbs into remote past tenses, it may be better to rephrase. Fig 6.3 records the metamorphosis of a Church Affairs Committee item from first live, overheated utterance to final, cool minute.

In practice, your notes will probably not look as streamlined as the Chairman's because you will tend to note items as you hear them. Much sifting and discarding will have to be done later. Minutes are not just a report or précis of proceedings: a great deal goes on at meetings which is not (and should not) be recorded!

6.6 The form of the minutes

All project-related (which usually means contract-related) meetings should be formally minuted. Special care should be taken where the meeting is critical – for example, the first site meeting or a meeting which concerns the determination of a contract. The minutes may become essential evidence if there is a dispute subsequently.

It is up to you to decide what kind of record you make of other kinds of meetings. At some, the participants may take turns to 'write up some notes'. These may simply consist of headings under which progress and actions are noted. At others, such as a brainstorming or a meeting called to generate an exchange of information, a very full (sometimes even verbatim) record will be needed, and it should be agreed in advance how this is to be done. In the case of a series of meetings, such as site or project meetings, the minutes establish continuity and provide a framework for discussion. They are also a valuable checklist to ensure that nothing is omitted.

A tripartite stratagem
The form of the meeting will influence the form of the minutes and the agenda. An example is where a client wishes to attend your site meetings but you would prefer him or her not to be present during your detailed and often distinctly down-to-earth discussions with the contractor. In these circumstances a three-part meeting may be a useful stratagem.

Part One is the usual contract meeting attended by the architect, consultants and contractor. The client joins the meeting for Part Two to hear the architect's report and to discuss various matters with all parties. The contractor then leaves and Part Three begins. This is where

FIG 6.3
Minuting a 'live' item at a meeting of the Church Affairs Committee, Chorley

(a) A fly on the wall

DR JAMES (Hon. Sec.):

'Chairman, could I draw the meeting's attention to a letter dated last Tuesday from Norman Bluff? I must say I think it's disgraceful. Quite scurrilous. Bluff is, and always has been in my opinion, an out and out troublemaker. Why, I think it was in 1978 – no, I tell a lie – it was 1979 that he actually had the gall to . . .

CHAIRMAN:

'Thank you, George, thank you. We all remember the incident vividly. Can we hear what the letter says, please?

DR JAMES:

'Er . . . yes . . . certainly, Chairman . . . um . . . here goes! "Dear James, I feel it is my duty to complain about the present state of St Agnes. Next month I will have been a side warden for thirty years, and in all that time I have never seen the church in such a poor state. No wonder the congregations are small, what with broken pews, wilting flowers, a leaking roof and graffiti on some of the columns. To crown it all, they have to endure Mr Noble's pathetic attempts to play the organ. He shouldn't be allowed near a barrel organ, let alone the valuable Hoffnungst which my dear wife used to play for many eloquent years before her illness. I see that there are new and significant cracks in the stained glass window near the organ loft. Need I say more? As for his attempt last Sunday to render a toccata by Peter Maxwell Davies – well, it not only distressed the congregation (Mrs Peacock left the service quite pointedly, I thought, before the collection), it has decimated the wildlife in the churchyard. Not a robin sings, even the magpies have taken flight. The man is an environmental hazard. Something must be done about it, and I hope you will raise this matter at your next committee meeting. Yours sincerely, Norman Bluff."

CHAIRMAN:

'Thank you, Dr James. Well — ! I must say he has a point about the toccata – I wish Mr Noble would stick to Handel. However, perhaps we should remember that Norman Bluff has been a loyal servant of this church for many years, and it's only since his wife became ill that he's been so touchy. Yes, Miss Grebe?

(continued)

Fig 6.3 *(continued)*

CECILIA GREBE:

'Chairman, may I comment on the environmental aspect? The reason for the departure of the birds probably has more to do with the recent increase of F1–11 training flights from the base at Apthorp. They always seem to fly directly over the church spire – I think they use it as a landmark – and some of the flights seem to be very low. The vibrations *may* have been sufficient to cause cracks in the windows, but I would have to take expert advice to be sure.

CHAIRMAN:

'Quite so. Thank you, Miss Grebe. As a first step, I think we ought to complain about the increase in F1–11s overhead. Does everyone agree that the Hon. Sec. should write a letter to Apthorp and suggest that they vary their training circuit? Very well. Dr James, would you kindly draft a suitable letter? Oh, and please write to Norman Bluff and tell him that we have noted his letter, will you?'

(b)   The Chairman's notes of the item

JAMES:

Read out letter from Bluff (29 May): 'poor condition of church - pews, flowers, graffiti, leaking roof. Bad effect on congregations. Mr N's awful shot at toccata. Cracks in sgw near organ loft. Wildlife decimated (!). Do something.'
(NB: visit Mrs B in hospital)

GREBE:

Wildlife and (possibly) sgw problems due to increased F1-11s overflying.

ACTION

Hon sec to write to airbase. And ack B's letter. RR to look into cleaning and flowers.

(continued)

Fig 6.3 (*continued*)

(c) The minuted item

7   ANY OTHER BUSINESS

   7.1 Letter from Norman Bluff

   The Hon. Sec. read out a letter from Norman Bluff dated
   29 May 19-- drawing attention to the church's poor
   state of repair and upkeep. He was particularly
   concerned about new cracks in the stained glass window
   near the organ loft, and the disappearance of wildlife
   from the churchyard.

   Miss Grebe commented that the departure of wildlife was
   probably the result of the recent increase in F1-11
   training flights out of the Apthorp air base, many of
   which overflew the church at low altitude. Without
   expert advice, she could not be sure whether this had
   also caused the cracks in the stained glass window. It
   was agreed that the Hon. Sec. should write a letter of
   complaint to Apthorp and ask them to vary their
   training circuits. The Hon. Sec. would also acknowledge
   Mr Bluff's letter and assure him that the matters he
   had raised were being investigated. Mr Redford agreed
   to report back on current arrangements for cleaning the
   church and arranging the flowers.
   Action: GJ, RR

---

the client can speak his mind freely to the architect out of earshot of
the contractor. A typical agenda for a tripartite meeting is given as Fig
6.4. The minutes of the various parts may be combined or separated
for distribution at the architect's discretion.

6.7 Issuing the minutes

Minutes should be issued as soon as possible after a meeting. If it is
imperative to get them drafted, typed and despatched the following
day, it will probably mean that you have to drop everything else.
Otherwise, aim at sending them out not more than three days after

FIG 6.4
Agenda for a tripartite meeting

Name of project   Job no.

Type of meeting   Meeting no.

This meeting will be held at Sparrow and Grebe's offices on
(date). Please notify absences etc to (name) at this office.

The meeting is to be held in three parts:

   10:30   1 Architect and contractor - site meeting
   11:15   2 All parties - report to client
   11:30   3 Client and architect - progress meeting
             and any other business

A G E N D A

1	2	3
Minutes		
Matters arising		
Contractor's report: progress and programme		
Sub-contractors		
Instructions and information required		
Any other business		
	<u>Client joins</u> Architect's report	
	Discussion	
	Date of next meeting <u>Contractor leaves</u>	
		Relevant minutes
		Matters arising
		Discussion
		Any other business

Date (agenda was issued):

Distribution:

the meeting. Apart from looking impressively efficient, the quicker you get the minutes out the more time people have to take the action or obtain the information required of them, and the more likely they are to make a satisfactory contribution to the next meeting. This includes the architect-cum-chairperson-cum-secretary!

6.8 Meetings of experts

Evidence of opinion

Architects are sometimes required to act as expert witnesses in litigation. This does not necessarily imply outstanding expertise in any particular subject; within the law it means that the court will recognise the ability of a witness with knowledge and experience in a particular field to give evidence of *opinion*, whereas other witnesses are restricted to giving evidence of *fact*. The role and function of the expert witness in the context of report writing is discussed in 7.8.

The court will make an order which sets a timetable for conducting the proceedings and includes a date by which a meeting (or meetings) of experts must be held, and a later date on which the parties must exchange the reports of their respective experts.

An 'agreed minute'

The purpose of a meeting of experts is to identify any items in the Plaintiff's claim which can be agreed and settled by negotiation rather than be allowed to proceed to (or, once the trial has started, to continue in) litigation. For example, it may be possible to agree liability for certain alleged defects and amounts for remedial measures. To this end the Court requires an agreed minute of the meeting to be prepared. This should be brief and to the point, noting only those items of the Statement of Claim or Scott Schedule upon which there is or is not agreement or, in multi-party actions, which parties agree or disagree on each item of claim. A draft agreed minute is prepared by the person in the chair, usually the plaintiff's expert, and is distributed to the other experts for comment and amendment. Once agreement is reached, it is signed by all the experts for the benefit of the Court.

Very occasionally the experts' meeting consists of a series of sub-meetings. In these circumstances it is desirable for full minutes to be taken of each sub-meeting to form aides-mémoire which will help the experts to formulate an agreed minute at the end of the process.

6.9 A final word from Sir Humphrey

Someone unwisely alleged that Sir Humphrey's minutes failed to record a (subsequently inconvenient) decision taken at a meeting. His reply was masterly.

'It is characteristic of committee discussions and decisions that every member has a vivid recollection of them and that every member's recollection differs violently from every other member's recollection. Consequently we accept the convention that the official decisions were those and only those which are officially recorded in the minutes by the officials, from which it follows with an elegant inevitability that any decision officially reached will be officially recorded in the minutes and any decision not recorded in the minutes was not officially reached even if one or more members believe that they recollect it. So in this particular case, if the decision had been officially reached it would have been officially recorded by the officials in the minutes. And . . . it isn't, so it wasn't.'

[Extract from *Yes, Prime Minister* by Anthony Jay and Jonathan Lynn, BBC Books 1986; copyright the authors.]

Section 7

Writing reports

It is quite apparent that because the gutter has been
laid with a reverse fall, because of the building being
out of level, that the leakage into the building is
exacerbated ...

(Anon)

Reports may be associated with various aspects of building design and construction and its environment; as well as architects, they may be written by solicitors, engineers, surveyors, planners, interior designers and specialist consultants of various kinds.

The important point to remember about reporting of any kind is that it essentially consists of

- presenting facts for information;
- interpreting them, and if asked to do so,
- suggesting and comparing solutions (for development or remedy);
- making recommendations.

Reports are not the form of communication in which to request information or action. They may *provoke* a response, but that is not the same thing. Whenever a reply is needed, a covering letter should be written.

7.1 Keeping the client informed

The type of report likely to be most familiar to architects is a progress report to client connected with a building project. Project-related reports may be about feasibility (Stage B of the *Plan of Work*), outline proposals (Stage C), scheme design (Stage D) and then the regular progress reports required to keep the client informed and to ask for approval to proceed to the next stage. Separate financial reports may have to be presented if there is no quantity surveyor appointed for the project (see the *Architect's Job Book* for examples).

Progress reports vary in shape and size according to the complexity and nature of the project; in its later stages, 'reports' may be better written as letters, especially where approval is being requested or a specific answer is urgently required. Recipients of reports tend to regard them as the answers to questions rather than as a vehicle for posing them.

Some clients insist on being sent copies of site meeting minutes, but this does not necessarily mean that they will pick up from the minutes the information that you expect them to, and they may even be confused by some of the technical items. Therefore it is unwise to rely on minutes as a medium for keeping clients properly informed.

It is essential to report events arising under the building contract promptly and to make sure that the client understands their implications fully.

FEASIBILITY REPORTS

Feasibility reports are often difficult to structure because they need to present a great deal of information in an easily digestible way to allow the client to make a properly informed decision about whether to proceed. They typically consist of a number of options, and these should be clearly set out, discussed and costed as accurately as possible. The formal report structure, discussed in detail in 7.3, can be modified and used for this kind of report.

INSPECTIONS OF PROPERTY

Reports of inspections of property of various kinds can take the form of investigative reports, but are more usefully presented as schedules, and there are many published forms which make this task easier. The structure which has been built into them helps the person reporting to organise the often formidable amount of detail so that nothing is overlooked.

7.2 Formal reports

It helps to think of a report as the considered answer to a question. It may be that someone is prepared to commission you to provide that answer, in which case this is a business transaction and you are required to give someone value for money. Alternatively, you may wish to propound your views on some aspect of professional or practice policy, or to explain your past actions which may be under scrutiny and you decide to do so in the form of a report.

In the case of a commission, it is likely that a letter will come in addressed to someone in particular rather than to the practice in general. This is often because the addressee has a good reputation as a writer or has some expert knowledge of or expertise in a particular field. If pressure of work or imminent holidays means that he or she is unable to accept the commission, then the letter may arrive on *your* desk with an 'Over to you!' note on it.

Reports commissions are formally accepted in writing and their cost is negotiated and agreed, usually on a time-charge basis, although research reports may be commissioned on a lump sum basis for the total project. Their contents are the property of the person who has commissioned them and are confidential. Confidentiality is very important where commercial confidence is a prerequisite or where the report concerns an investigation into perceived or alleged defects which may subsequently give rise to litigation (see 7.8).

Organising the work

Only accept a commission, whether on your own or someone else's behalf, when you have fully considered the implications in terms of staff effort and availability and what knock-on effects there may be on other work in progress.

When you do accept a commission, you must plan a programme of work within a timescale. This may be imposed by the client's requirements or reflect your own assessment of the amount of your time that the fee will buy at your charge-out rate.

A common error is to underestimate the time required for preparing the report as opposed to making any investigation leading to it. This is because, perhaps naturally, many architects regard investigation as the 'real' job and writing the report as a necessary 'chore' tacked on at the end. Reports commissions are time-consuming, especially for the inexperienced: copious notes relating to photographs, tests and inspections have to be taken on site, and then back in the office the drafting, revising and final editing of the report is a long and often exhausting process.

It helps if you keep the structure and purpose of the report in your mind from the earliest stages of the investigation so that you can organise your notes in a suitable form and draft some sections during the investigation period rather than leave everything to the end.

7.3 The structure of reports

A standard report structure is given as Fig 7.0. This is the logical and recognised way to organise information that is being given as the reply to a question about a set of facts. The discipline of the formal

```
FIG 7.0
Typical structure of a formal report
------------------------------------------------------------------
Cover
            Title page
            Contents list
Summary of report*
Glossary*

            1.0  Introduction

            1.1  The brief
            1.2  Background information
            1.3  Scope of report
            1.4  Methodology
Site/building plans*, area maps*
Press cuttings*
Divider    -----------------------------------------------------

            2.0  Findings

            2.1
            2.2  etc
            2.3  Summary
Figures*
Photographs*
Divider    -----------------------------------------------------

            3.0  Conclusions and recommendations

            3.1  Conclusions
            3.2  Recommendations
Divider    -----------------------------------------------------

            4.0  Remedial proposals (if required)

            4.1  Options available
            4.2  Costs
            4.3  Recommendations
Figures*, Tables*
Divider    -----------------------------------------------------
            References*
            Appendices*
            May include photographs, published technical
            information, validating correspondence, trade
            literature etc
Divider    -----------------------------------------------------
            Bibliography*
            Index*
Cover
------------------------------------------------------------------
Add any separate accompanying items.
* Variables (see 7.3)
```

report structure does not have to be unyielding at all costs. If you find that the information you want to present *doesn't* fit into the standard format exactly and you need to add or vary sections and elements, then you should do so. But the structure overall must remain logical and coherent.

Each element of the main text has a specific purpose and function as part of the total argument and it helps to understand what these are. In addition, every report must have a title page and contents list. Then there are a number of variable items (asterisked in Fig 7.0) which can be included in the report's preliminaries or form part of its end matter. All these are now described under their respective headings.

Main text

(1) INTRODUCTION
The introductory section establishes the terms of reference for the report, gives relevant background information to put it in context, defines its scope and describes the way the investigation has been tackled.

(1.1) THE BRIEF
The instructions from the client constitute the terms of reference for the report. They answer questions such as:

Who is this report for?
Why is it being commissioned?
What is it about?
When is it to be presented?
Who will be writing it?

There may also be instructions about how it should be presented. In the course of writing the report, re-read its terms of reference to keep your thinking focused and relevant. This is sometimes not easy when side issues seem more interesting than the main study.

It is usual to include an account of the commissioning process in this section, on the following lines:

EXAMPLE:
On (date) we were instructed by Mr E C Jay, Estates Officer for the ABC Development Bureau, to carry out an investigation of . . . and present our findings as a draft report to be submitted to the Central Housing Committee on (date) . . . . We accepted this

commission by letter on (date) saying that the investigation would be
made by Peregrine Sparrow DipArch and Cecilia Grebe DipArch.

Copies of the exchange of commissioning letters are sometimes
included in an Appendix. Note that expert reports for litigation
are differently presented (see 7.8).

(1.2) BACKGROUND INFORMATION

This sub-section is also sometimes called *History of the Project*. As you
might imagine, it is where the writer fills in the reader with relevant
background information about why the report has been commissioned,
so that he or she can read it in proper context. For example, the report
might be about an unpopular housing estate where there had been a
long history of vandalism and neglect and where many attempts had
been made to mitigate its problems. It would be relevant to say what
these problems are or were, what solutions were tried out, by whom
and to what effect. It might be appropriate to include a map of the
locality.

(1.3) SCOPE OF REPORT

This sub-section states the extent of the report in physical terms.

EXAMPLE:
The report covers all the two-storey terraced dwellings in Phases
1 and 2 of the development, but excludes all the 3-storey dwellings
in Phase 2. It was agreed (with the client) *that the extensive*
condensation observed in many of the flats should be the subject of a
separate report.

A site or building plan could be included to identify the different areas.

(1.4) METHODOLOGY

This is where you say how you tackled the investigation and what
actions you took. For example, you may have made three visits to site.
Describe them in chronological order, saying who was present at each,
what you did, whether tests were made and if so why, where and by
whom. Add whether you or others carried out any supporting research
(for example into local history, social conditions, climate, water tables
etc). If you have added any appendices say why and in what respect
they may be useful to readers.

Then briefly describe how you have organised the material in
the report.

EXAMPLE:

This report consists of four main sections. In section 1 we describe the events which led to this commission and the way we have tackled the work. Section 2 records our findings, and Section 3 sets out the conclusions we deduce and our recommendations for action. In Section 4 we discuss the remedial solutions available, and compare and cost the proposed options. We conclude this section with recommendations. The appendices contain items and information which support and validate our findings and recommendations.

(2) FINDINGS

The findings should be a clear statement of facts. You invite the reader to observe them just as you observed them. Resist the temptation to throw in remarks or draw early conclusions or propose solutions. This is where you are truly the reporter.

This section of the report will go into some detail, breaking down the inspection of a building into, say, an element-by-element description (preferably illustrated). It will say who was present during the survey, what the weather conditions were then and had been recently (eg heavy rain the night before). It will record in detail opening-up procedures, borescope inspections, dye or spray tests and so on. Some photographs may be included, but if they are numerous it is probably better to present them in an appendix.

Because of the technical detail included it is useful to conclude the section with a *Summary of Findings* and to illustrate the material wherever possible. One good illustration can give the reader more information than several pages of text. Architects, in spite of being essentially visual people, are remarkably shy about including visual information in reports. Few clients are dedicated readers; they yearn for drawings, tables, plans, maps and photographs to help them along.

(3) CONCLUSIONS AND RECOMMENDATIONS

It is when you set about analysing the situation that the facts reveal and the existing or potential problems they suggest that you the reporter must become you the expert. After analysing the situation you will draw conclusions (3.1) and then, if you have been asked to do so in the brief, suggest courses of future action, explaining the salient aspects of various alternatives and the financial and other implications (3.2).

Set out your conclusions clearly as itemised points. State the options available as *(a)*, *(b)*, *(c)* etc so that you can refer to them thereafter as *Option (a)* etc without having to recapitulate them extensively.

Some investigative reports end at this point. Where the brief asks for proposals for remedial solutions, another part is added.

(4) REMEDIAL PROPOSALS
The options you describe (4.1) and cost and compare (4.2) will have been chosen because of their suitability within the context of any budget. Recommendations (4.3) must be performable as well as cost-effective, and it is essential at this stage to draw attention to any limitations or disadvantages of the remedies you are proposing.

Title page, contents list
Every report must have a title page and a list of contents.

TITLE PAGE
Regardless of any pre-printed information given on the cover (see 7.9) each report should include a title page which shows its title and job number, status (draft, interim, final etc), date, and the name and address of the client. Covers often become detached with handling or during storage and may be lost. As a result, the report may be difficult to identify, particularly if a considerable time has elapsed since it was written or if it was one of a series. Therefore it is commonsense to include full information about the report's origination on the title page and at the very end of the text after the appropriate signatures. Give the initials of the writer *and* the typist, followed by the job or reference number and the date, eg BL/HM/475/20.7.89.

CONTENTS LIST
All the contents of the report should be noted, including the Appendices, Figures, Tables, References and Bibliography. It is helpful to list the figures and tables fully with the title of each as well as its number.

Variables – preliminary items

SUMMARY OF REPORT
A separate summary of findings, conclusions and recommendations is sometimes attached to the front of the report immediately after the title page. This is not often appropriate for short reports but can be useful where the report is lengthy, makes numerous recommendations, or is for the use of a committee. In the very rare case of the report's findings

100

being part of a *cause célèbre* such a summary could be used as a handout for the Press.

A *Summary of report* is a 'convenience' item for at-a-glance information. It is not *part* of the report and should only repeat given information. It can be written in the third person, rather as if it were a news item, and should be no longer than a page.

EXAMPLE:
Summary of report

Following complaints from tenants on the ABC Estate *about deteriorating living conditions, in July 19— (the client) commissioned Sparrow and Grebe to investigate (the condition of the dwellings) and propose remedial solutions. In the Phase 1 terraced dwellings they discovered extensive evidence of water penetration, and some evidence of damp in the bathrooms and kitchens of the Phase 2 flats.*

The terraced properties require major repairs. Remedial options have been compared and costed, and the alternatives recommended are (a) to . . . or (b) to . . . . Option (b) entails significantly lower maintenance costs than option (a).

The relatively minor condensation problems in the flats can be mitigated by simple improvements to the air extract system and by modifying the ventilation grilles.

GLOSSARY

When a report contains numerous specialist or technical terms, it is helpful to include a glossary to explain them. It should appear at the front of the report, usually just after the contents list, so that the reader is immediately reassured that linguistic salvation is at hand. List the items alphabetically and make sure that the explanations *are* explanations in plain non-technical English. Don't frame them in such a way that your readers will return to the original with relief!

Variables – end matter

REFERENCES

Publications or sources of information are often referred to in the body of the report. Each item should be given a number (superscribed or in brackets), and a related list of numbered references should follow immediately after the main text. it may be convenient to use footnotes for references while you are drafting your report, but in the final version the *readers'* convenience is paramount and a separate list is generally more useful.

APPENDICES

Although nothing crucial to the theme should be banished into an appendix, it is important not to clutter up the main text with extraneous material. A sudden encounter with three pages of statistics will not make your readers warm to your arguments. In some reports you may need to include copies of relevant correspondence, notices, extracts from codes and standards or related literature, even translations of learned foreign research papers on occasion. These can all be included as appended items.

Appendices should be listed on the Contents page at the front of the report. Each should have its own title page and number and its own internal page numbering. Paragraphs should be numbered in a similar style to the main text, with appropriate prefixes (*A1, A2, B1, B2*).

Appendices should include material that *supports* the main text. Always try to keep the main text as short as possible, fluent and easy to read.

BIBLIOGRAPHY

In the context of report-writing, a bibliography is a list of sources of information consulted by the author in the course of preparing a report. It is a category of information in its own right and should be kept separate from appendices. Sometimes more than one kind of bibliography is appropriate: for example, a selected bibliography may be appropriate support for the main text, whilst a detailed bibliography may be needed for a topic discussed in detail in an appendix. In other cases, a list of publications recommended for general information may be sufficient.

Reports which have required extensive literature searches or are research-based must have full bibliographies to validate them. More detailed advice on research reports and academic presentations can be found in the *RIBA Dissertation Handbook* by Peter Willis (1983).

INDEX

An index is indispensable where there are numerous topics which a reader might want to pick out for special attention (in this book, for example), but technical reports rarely require one because their scope of enquiry is relatively limited. If an index is desirable, it should be the very last item included in the report.

7.4 Judging the readers' level of knowledge

'Words are the foes of reality.'

(Joseph Conrad)

If you underestimate the level of knowledge of your readers, much of what you are saying will be superfluous; overestimate it and you may be unintelligible. Your choice of terminology should relate closely to their supposed level of knowledge. Remember that professional jargon (see 1.3) is often gobbledegook to a lay person.

In practice, you will often have to steer a middle course, particularly where the client is a committee consisting of, say, members of various professions, local authority officers and lay people. These latter may be the users of the subject of the investigation (such as tenants or their representatives), so that it is particularly important that they should understand fully what you are talking about. These are the kind of circumstances where it may be useful to write a *Summary of report.*

A good habit, whatever the level and kind of readership expected, is to sum up at the end of sections in the main text, particularly where the subject matter is complex or technical. For example, after describing in detail the condition of the windows in a block of flats, in the course of which you may refer to dpm's, reveals, overhangs, primary/secondary/tertiary glazing, string courses, rwo's, site topography, the Driving Rain Index and 'severe events', you could simply add:

To sum up, in typically wet and windy conditions, all the west-facing windows leaked around the frames.

7.5 Writing the report

It is still maintained in some quarters that all reports should be written in the strictly observational style of formal scientific reporting:

The liquid was observed to boil. It was concluded that . . .

This is a hangover from the days when this style of writing was adopted to demonstrate the total impartiality of the reporter; unfortunately it came to be favoured whenever anyone wanted to write 'seriously' about anything. It is old-fashioned, tedious and unwieldy.

In report writing special efforts have to be made to achieve an appropriate style of writing: one that is clear and unequivocal, businesslike, free of subjective judgments, reactions and 'asides', and suited to the disciplined structure of the report format. The linguistic peccadilloes and inelegances that sometimes characterise practice correspondence will not be overlooked or forgiven if they appear in reports. They will erode the validity of the opinions expressed and do little to reassure the client of the excellence of the writer's professional judgment. Here are some reminders.

Aim at a clear and fluent style
Report writers should try to achieve a fluent style of writing free from literary devices, jargon and clichés (see 3.7).

BE BUSINESSLIKE

Your tone should be consistently helpful and pleasant, neither chatty at one end of the formality scale, nor clinically remote at the other. Do not pontificate or lecture your readers. Decide how to refer to yourself as the author of the report. The safest advice is always to use *we*, meaning your firm, except in expert reports for litigation (see 7.8).

BE CONCISE AND ACCURATE

Remove weak modifiers such as *quite, rather, somewhat, about*. To say that *the bricks were rather/somewhat/wet* tells the reader nothing about the *degree* of wetness, just that the bricks were wet. Similarly, prune out monitoring phrases such as *as it were, so it seems, all things being equal, to all intents and purposes, more or less*. Thoughtless use of these can weaken or actually defeat what you are trying to say, see Fig 1.0:

'I recommended some improvements, for better or worse.'

BE SPECIFIC

Generalities (see 3.4) such as *Flashings generally blow off in bad weather* are not going to help anyone and will make you look foolish. Beware of making value judgments (subjective estimates of quality), such as *This is a good way to fix tiles, The contractor made a bad decision*. In reports in particular, statements should be validated.

BE RELEVANT

Do not include superfluous or distracting themes and details. As a check while you are working on the report, re-read the brief at the end of each section and ask yourself whether what you have written is useful and relevant. Keep to the point.

BE INTELLIGIBLE

If you cannot avoid using unfamiliar, specialist terms, make sure that you add explanations where necessary, and take care to sum up frequently in plain English. Include a glossary of terms at the front of the report, if necessary.

BE DIGESTIBLE

The more difficult a subject is to grasp, the more important it is to present material in appetising chunks by making paragraph breaks at logical points in the argument or discussion. Regard with deep suspicion any paragraph that consists of only one sentence. If it is short, it should probably be joined on to the preceding or following paragraph. If it is long, it is probably unintelligible and needs splitting up. Paragraph headings relieve the monotony of a long text and help readers find specific topics. Make sure that they are relevant and keep them short.

When in doubt, rephrase
Many linguistic knots can be untied by rephrasing sentences (or whole passages) instead of trying to find a precise change of word or construction. You can 'free' a dense sentence by introducing more clauses and sentence division.

EXAMPLE:

(a) *Built in 1932, Hoopers Park, a Tudor-style development with houses arranged around a central courtyard, was recently designated a Grade II listed building.*

(b) *The Hoopers Park development was built in 1932. The houses, which are Tudor-style, are arranged around a central courtyard. Hoopers Park has recently been designated a Grade II listed building.*

7.6 Checking the report

There are three stages of checking needed: your own work, the typed version of the report, and lastly the way the material has been assembled and presented.

First check: before typing
Before sending the draft for typing, ask yourself:

> *Have I answered the brief adequately?*
> *Have I said what I meant to say?*
> *Will the reader understand this report?*
> *Are the conclusions/recommendations clearly set out?*

Go somewhere quiet and read the report out loud. This is an effective way of exposing lack of fluency and clarity of expression. Alternatively,

105

ask a colleague to read it through and tell you if there is anything that he or she doesn't understand.

Second check: before binding

Before photocopying and binding, check:

- for typing and spelling errors;
- that the report looks well-presented;
- that the contents list corresponds with the actual contents, paragraph numbers and headings and that page numbers have been inserted;
- that all the items to be included are assembled in the proper order;
- that the report has been signed, dated and referenced.

Before photocopying, a report must always be signed and dated by the writer at the end of the main text and, with the exception of expert reports, be countersigned by one of the partners or directors, who is thereby assumed to have read the report and approved its contents. Time is short in architectural practice, but it is essential that this really happens. It has been known for a practice to be separately commissioned to present expert advice on behalf of opposing parties and for this, mercifully, to have been picked up at that crucial final reading.

Third check: before despatch

Before despatch, check:

- that the right number of copies has been prepared (remembering to allow for the requirements of the filing system, library etc and a working copy for yourself);
- that each copy has been correctly collated and no skewed or defective pages have been included;
- that the necessary identifying information has been included and is visible on the cover page;
- that the report handles well;
- that any separate packages of items have been properly prepared and are clearly marked as accompanying items.

This final checking must not be scamped: always allow plenty of time and don't ring up for a special messenger to come and collect until you have finished. Working under pressure is one thing – and architects are well accustomed to it – but *checking* must never be done in a hurry.

At this point, aglow with a sense of honest toil completed, you may feel justified in breathing a sigh of relief and taking the beagle for a long overdue walk. But in the real world, the task of writing a report is not always straightforward.

7.7 Problems arising

However conscientiously you plan your work on the report, there will be times when you will be unable to meet the deadline for submitting it. It may be because your researches lead you to realise that more investigation is necessary than you had anticipated, or because a testing laboratory informs you that they will need six weeks to report on samples instead of three. Sometimes you may simply have underestimated the time you would need to complete the commission, or followed a wrong path of enquiry, or some personal problem has cropped up and disturbed your concentration.

Whatever the reason, tell the client as early as possible about the delay. This is never easy, but having failed to meet the date set, on no account be panicked into trying to retrieve the situation by saying that you will do your best to have the report ready 'next week' if that is impossibly optimistic. Think out the situation carefully *before* giving the client the bad news, then take your courage in both hands, give the best explanation or excuse you can and suggest a realistic later date which you *can* meet.

It is very important to meet submission dates, especially in expert reports for the Court, but it is even more important to submit a *good* report, even if a little late, than a poor one on time.

A compromise

If some of the information is ready, such as your report on condition, you may be able to agree with the client that you will submit a preliminary report, on time, containing purely observational material. This will allow you to take stock of the situation, consult your colleagues or, if you think it is really necessary, make (further) tests or observations. It may be that for further checks you need to wait for a period of heavy rain or a severe overnight frost or to obtain some specialist advice from, say, a soil mechanics engineer.

Most clients will be reasonable if you are frank with them; after all, they want a real solution or statement from you – that's what they are paying for. But remember to agree the additional fees involved if you want to bring in outside help.

If you write a preliminary report of this kind, you must make this clear in the report. The report will be entitled *Preliminary* and will state in the *Scope of Report* section what is being left in abeyance for the time being, and the approximate time-scale for further reports. It will end after the *Findings* section, which will conclude with a brief statement of what actions you intend to take before making the recommendations that your readers are expecting. It is probably better not to state a specific date for submitting the next report, although you will certainly have to agree one with the client in an exchange of correspondence.

It may be that a report is commissioned in stages anyway. There may be a preliminary report, followed by an interim report, to be superseded eventually by a final report. The preliminary report may just state the findings, the interim may discuss the options available and explore and cost further alternatives, and the final report reviews the situation in the light of the reactions of the client and latest cost estimates, and makes final recommendations for action.

Naturally, in the best of all possible worlds, your evaluation will be thorough and will be made in good time so that potential problem areas can be anticipated and, with luck, avoided. But no one in real-life professional practice is likely to forget that they have to be ready to cope with crisis situations at any time.

7.8 Reports for litigation

Litigation is a legal process for resolving disputes. These may arise from breach of contract or statutory duty, or from negligence. It used to be rare for architects to be involved in litigation, but these days they are increasingly retained as expert witnesses in construction disputes.

The function of an expert witness is to assist a Court or an Inquiry to arrive at fair and just decisions. In Britain, the expert witness is not an advocate for the client: he or she has been retained to give independent and objective evidence.

To be accepted by the Court as an expert witness able to deal with the special issues in question you have to be able to demonstrate a special authority derived from qualification or experience.

An architect's involvement in litigation often starts with an instruction to report on the condition of a building in the standard form of report already described. He or she may sometimes be asked to give an opinion about the attribution of responsibilities for alleged defects.

On the basis of this first advisory report a client may decide to take legal action and to ask the architect-investigator to act as an expert witness once proceedings have been initiated. This is usually in the Queen's Bench Division of the High Court and the action is dealt with as Official Referee's business. The judge will have special jurisdiction to hear cases which involve complex technical matters.

Claims for professional negligence invariably involve expert evidence on both sides, because otherwise it cannot be proved (or disproved) whether the Defendant satisfied the standard adopted by his profession. As a result, solicitors have to be engaged to gather evidence and prepare the case and barristers are asked for opinions and may subsequently be retained for any trial – one of their tasks being to cross-examine the expert witnesses. As a result, the costs rise alarmingly. Actions where the stakes are high often involve numerous defendants from various trades and professions all attended by their respective legal representatives. Months, sometimes years, can be spent intermittently in court.

The legal procedures before trial

The legal procedures before trial can assist in bringing about a settlement, which is the usual objective.

The Court will issue an Order of Directions setting the timetable for the action, dates for experts on both sides to meet, and dates for exchanging expert reports (see 6.8). The Court may also make an order for the Discovery of Documents before trial.

'DISCOVERY'

This means that the parties to the dispute must disclose for the inspection of the other side all the relevant documents they hold which are not privileged. In the case of a building contract, this will include drawings, bills of quantities, instructions and certificates, minutes and correspondence files. Correspondence between solicitor and client, expert reports and proofs of evidence prepared for the purposes of the action are privileged.

Lists of the unprivileged documents are drawn up by both sides and the parties are given the opportunity to inspect any of the documents listed. Experts should make the inspection themselves, accompanied by their side's solicitors, and must consider in the light of their own inspection of the real evidence and the matters at issue whether the documents disclosed include all the information needed for the expert report; if they do not, then they may ask if there is further or other

FIG 7.1
A Scott Schedule

	STATEMENT OF CLAIM ITEM AND DESCRIPTION	LOCATION	PLAINTIFF'S REMEDIAL PROPOSALS	AMOU CLAI
5	ROOFING WORKS			
5(a)	Tiles not fixed in accordance with Bs of Qs, specification and manufacturer's instructions.			
5(b)	Tiles not fixed in accordance with relevant BS and CP.			
5(c)	Ridge tiles not well bedded and/or without solid bedded butt joints.			
5(d)	Eaves and top tile courses: tiles not mechanically fixed.			
5(e)	Verge and abutment tiles: some end course tiles not mechanically fixed.			
5(f)	Eave filler pieces missing or not used.			
5(g)	Nails of inadequate strength used and not driven sufficiently into battens.			

information which has not been listed. Copies of documents are usually supplied at cost.

Then follows the exacting and time-consuming task of going through all the documentation and identifying the items that are crucial to the expert report.

STATEMENT OF CLAIM

A Statement of Claim may have been served, followed by a Defence and Counterclaim and a Reply. A Scott Schedule (see below) may also have been served. It is helpful to relate items in the expert report to the Statement of Claim. Those in the Scott Schedule usually, though not always, follow the same sequence. Generally speaking, the expert witness will have been retained before the Statement of Claim or the

SCOTT SCHEDULE
Name of action:
Names of parties:

DEFENDANT'S ENTS *	ESTIMATE OF COSTS*	PLAINTIFF'S REPLY*	FOR USE BY REFEREE

*Repeat columns for second and other Defendants.

Scott Schedule or any other Pleadings are drafted and should take part in their drafting, since he or she will have to support them.

SCOTT SCHEDULE

The Scott Schedule (sometimes called a 'Referee's Schedule') is initiated by a Plaintiff. It allows all items in dispute to be listed in detail and the comments of the respective parties to be entered against them. It is a flexible form and can easily be adapted; this is particularly useful where there is a large amount of technical detail. Its use may be ordered by a judge or arbitrator or it may be used by agreement between the parties.

The Plaintiff enters details of the alleged defects, proposals for remedying them and the amounts claimed and sends the form to each Defendant to add comments. The schedule is then returned to the Plaintiff to enter replies. Fig 7.1 is an example Scott Schedule. Where there are numerous Defendants, the column pattern is replicated as necessary.

PROOF OF EVIDENCE

A Proof of Evidence is a formal written statement prepared by a solicitor in which someone sets out facts and matters which he or she can swear are within his or her personal and direct knowledge. By contrast, the expert report is evidence of opinion. Architects are sometimes required to supply a Proof of Evidence when their own professional competence is at issue.

Writing the expert report

Lawyers, particularly Counsel, may have a view about the way the expert report is structured and presented, but generally they are anxious that it should avoid giving any impression of being 'tailored' and prefer to leave it up to you. However, it is likely that the first draft will be revised a number of times before the final version emerges. You will then have to be prepared to hold your ground if you are cross-examined about its contents. The report should be validated by supporting documentary evidence, such as copies of extracts from codes or standards or relevant literature.

Reports by expert witnesses are usually written in the first person and signed by that person only, the expert recognised by the Court. For that reason countersigning by a partner is not appropriate and may even call into question the expert's claim to exclusive authorship. In other words, you're on your own!

PREAMBLE

Professional standing and experience add weight to the expert evidence given. At the beginning of the report the expert has to declare who he or she is and state qualifications and experience relevant to the action being brought. This preamble is usually written in the first person, and invariably is in the case of proofs of evidence.

EXAMPLE:
I am Cecilia Grebe, Partner of Sparrow and Grebe, architects and environmental consultants, of 42 Old Gasworks View, Chorley. I am retained as expert witness on behalf of . . . .

In 1970 I was awarded an Honours Diploma in Architecture at . . . etc. Give a résumé of qualifications, work experience and anything of particular relevance to this action.

The report will be structured in the usual way, beginning with details of the brief, background information and a description of the way the investigation was tackled. Then the items of claim and response should be listed in the order they appear on the Scott Schedule (if any) and comments given, followed by comments on the remedial work required and the related costs. Lastly the expert sets out his or her conclusions. A further report may be required later, after the expert has studied the other side's reports.

7.9 Presentation of reports

Reports may be an important element of a firm's output and an important aspect of its public image. The way reports are organised and presented will be influenced by the firm's 'house style' and details may be set out in the office manual, if there is one.

There may be special report paper, usually white A4 with the firm's name printed top right and *Report:* in the top lefthand corner, and standard report folders and cover sheets for different methods of binding. Reports should be instantly recognisable as part of the output of a particular firm, and it is worthwhile having card report covers pre-printed with the firm's name and address and logo, if any, or special labels made for sticking on to hard covers.

Collating the material

The most important consideration is usability: a report must handle well and all its contents must be easily visible. This means that lefthand margins must be particularly generous if the report is tightly bound at the spine. Here are three popular solutions.

PLASTIC SLIDES
Plastic spine slides are often used for short draft reports and are easy to fit and labour-saving, but they do not open flat and the material they enclose is not easy to handle if major revisions need to be made. What usually happens is that the user removes the slide and threads

the pages together with a treasury tag to allow him or her to annotate the draft more easily.

SPIRAL BINDERS

Spiral binding is suitable for most reports apart from the very slim, but it is a more time-consuming process and if there has to be a re-draft the product is awkward to pull apart and reassemble. Usability is excellent, as the report can be opened completely flat and illustrative material such as photographs can be seen properly. It is a good way to present the final version of a report.

RING BINDERS AND LEVER-ARCH FILES

These are convenient for re-drafting purposes, and suitable for final reports, which are well protected by the hard covers. Final reports look well-presented if the folders are a standard colour and have pre-printed labels which show the firm's name and logo and can have the report title and job number typed on them. Late revisions, which often have to be made to litigation reports, are easy to make. Pages can be substituted and dividers used to identify different sections and appendices. The main drawback of this type of file is its bulkiness in handling and storage.

Report covers

Pre-printed A3 folded card covers are often used for draft reports where the text is stapled to the cover or the whole arrangement is gripped by a plastic slide.

For spiral-bound reports, covers could be in white card of about 300gsm, preferably glossy one side, to improve durability and 'feel' (and to fend off sticky fingers). Card can be laminated for a high gloss finish, ie it is given a plastic film. This is more expensive than using semi-glossy card such as Astralux, where the gloss is part of the manufacturing process. Most glossy finishes are difficult to type on, so it is a good idea for pre-printed front covers to have cut-out 'windows', to show the name of the report typed on the title page of the report inside (see *Title page*, 7.3).

If the card covers are exactly A4 and the sheets of report paper are exactly A4, however hard you try you will not get an even effect with spiral binding. To avoid this, you could specify a special size slightly larger than A4 when ordering your report covers.

Some firms believe in investing heavily in facilities for binding reports, brochures and booklets, and may buy one of the 'hot glue' machines.

There is no doubt that the results look professional, but bulky reports often don't stand up to vigorous handling and the techniques involved in the binding process take some time to perfect. For occasional special reports where a professional appearance is critical (and time permits) it might be more cost-effective to put the work out to a printer or one of the collect-and-deliver firms that service drawing offices.

Including awkward items

Problems can arise when putting a report together where there are different kinds of material to be included. For example, there may be sheets of photographs and these do not photocopy well, particularly if they are in colour. You may therefore have to assemble several sets of prints and mount them by hand. Use a light card rather than report paper, which may tear with the weight of the photograph. Captions can be typed on to the card, provided it is light enough, or typed on to sticky paper and applied in strips. Alternatively you could:

- make up one set of photographs and have each page re-photographed, including captions, or
- use plastic photograph wallets.

Another difficulty is where you have to include a large site plan or map or drawing which cannot be reduced to A4 without becoming unintelligible. Careful folding is necessary to make sure that it is included tidily within the report and that the reader is able to open it out properly. A3 drawings can be folded in neatly but, as with all folded items, the fold must be clear of the binding mechanism down the spine. Try not to include more than one or two foldouts, as they are inevitably bulky and become more so with use, spoiling the appearance of the report.

Any items difficult to bind into the report could accompany it in a separate folder or large envelope. Sometimes it is appropriate to put them in a plastic wallet and bind this into the report as an appendix.

7.10 Processing reports

Before the advent of the word processor there used to be much argument about whether reports should be typed in double or single spacing. The standard answer is stick to double spacing whenever the report has 'draft' status, or is likely to need re-drafting by any of the parties involved. Reports commissioned by the legal profession should always be double-spaced and it is best to ask for advice about what numbering system to adopt. Very often the answer is to number each and every paragraph throughout the draft in sequential whole numbers.

However, some clients may ask for the final versions of their reports to be presented single-spaced (or one-and-a-half), thinking that this looks more professional. This will reduce the size of a bulky report, and so will 'backing up' the pages (ie using both sides of the paper). In that case there are three important practical considerations:

- Centre the text so that it doesn't matter whether pages are finally left or righthand.
- Use paper of sufficient weight to allow the text to appear cleanly on both sides.
- Begin each section of the report on a new page, so that extra material can be inserted without disturbing the whole report. (But remember that additions are likely to affect the page numbering.)

Changing from double to single spacing and centering the text is easy enough to manage if the report has been keyed into a word processor. The wp is to be thoroughly recommended to architects who are regularly required to write reports. It is an extremely efficient tool for editing and revising and takes much of the pain out of those eleventh hour amendments, whether yours or the client's.

7.11 Feedback of information

As a practice develops so its library of reports will develop. It is often forgotten that this collection of researched information is a valuable asset which all professional and technical staff should be encouraged to share and study. Most architects would agree that in the course of preparing and researching a report they often encounter some new state of the art information or discover a fresh perspective on a problem, or find the solution to some aspect of design which they had never considered before.

None of this information should be allowed to disappear from the collective memory of the practice or, for that matter, to be lost to the building industry as a whole. Success will depend on whether the practice has an effective system for *disseminating*, as well as collecting information.

Section 8

Miscellaneous

8.1 Memos and notices

Most offices suffer from a proliferation of paper. Writing a lengthy memo to someone sitting in his or her office only a few paces away is a waste of time and effort if the matter can be sorted out in five minutes of discussion. Only resort to the written word when it is necessary and appropriate.

You may well have good reasons for doing so. For example, you may want to record your views in a form that can be kept pending, copied and circulated to others, tabled at a meeting and ultimately filed. Another good reason for going on record is that if the subject is controversial or concerns a grievance, writing it all down tends to take the steam out of the situation so that you can more easily set out a logical and persuasive argument. It also spares you and the addressee the ordeal of personal confrontation. It is difficult to remain calm and objective when you can *see* the reactions of the person you are addressing.

Notifying matters to the office *en masse* is always difficult. Architectural work requires staff to be absent from the office frequently, sometimes for days at a time, and when they *are* in they are usually too busy to look at the notice board and only the shortest of notes placed on their desks will be read. No urgent communication should ever consist of more than half a page of A4, or look like a memo; the memo format (Fig 8.0) is irretrievably connected in most people's minds with non-urgent matters. Use a notice format, plenty of headings and short, sharp sentences (as Fig 8.1).

To sum up, use notices to communicate urgent matters of information. They can soon be thrown away. Use memos for communicating non-urgent matters connected with office administration, staff and policy matters. These may be filed as appropriate.

8.2 Keeping records

Using forms helps to ensure that information is systematically recorded. Fig. 8.0 gives headings for Memorandum, Note to File and Record of

```
FIG 8.0
Headings for three office record forms
-----------------------------------------------------------------

1     Office Memorandum form

MEMORANDUM

      To:

      From:

      SUBJECT:                           Job/file no:

      Copy to:

      Date:

-----------------------------------------------------------------

2    Note to File form

NOTE TO FILE

      SUBJECT:                           Job/file no:

      Note by:

      Date:

      Copies to:

-----------------------------------------------------------------

3    Record of Telephone Call form

RECORD OF TELEPHONE CALL                 Date:

      With (name):
           (firm):
           (tel. no.):

      SUBJECT:                           Job/file no:
```

```
                        +---------------------------------------+
                        | Action required ...............       |
                        | ...............................       |
                        |                                       |
                        | Keep pending/file                     |
                        |                                       |
                        | Job/file no. .................        |
                        |                                       |
                        | Copy to .....................         |
                        +---------------------------------------+
```

Any of these record forms could have an Actions etc box inset like this one.

FIG 8.1
Notice about test of fire alarm

!ALL STAFF PLEASE NOTE!

TEST OF FIRE ALARM TODAY 12 FEBRUARY 1989
BETWEEN 12 NOON AND 14:00

Our new fire alarm system is being tested today
between 12 noon and 14:00.

There will be three tests. Each will consist of a
5-second ear-splitting electronic blast.

Do not panic! Do not initiate standard fire drill
procedures! But please remember another time that
this is the noise that means 'FIRE!'

Gloria Transit
(Office Manager)

Telephone Call forms for recording items, events, visits and background information that are job- or practice-related. All these may be copied to others for action or information before filing. The most convenient vehicle for recording essential project facts and events is the *Job Record* pad of forms, which is part of the *Architect's Job Book*. Remember, if you are inventing your own, that forms will only be used if they are kept simple. Don't be tempted to include too many detailed headings.

8.3 Forms for contract administration

Please note that Instruction No.12 dated 7th June 1986
will remain as Instruction No.12 while Instruction
No.12 without a date will become Instruction No.13;
please put the date as 9th June 1986. Instruction No.13
dated 12th June will now become Instruction No.14.

(Anon)

Building contracts refer to the issue of instructions, valuations, certificates etc, but seldom stipulate what form these should take. For example, in certain circumstances letters can be construed as instructions or even certificates. It is wise to agree at the outset with the parties concerned the form of important communications.

A range of contract administration forms for use with JCT contracts has been drafted by the RIBA Practice Department and published by RIBA Publications which, used properly, can help to reduce the risk of error and ambiguity. Letters will still be needed where, say, the architect is simply consenting to a proposal by the contractor, or where a warning is being given. But whenever you are communicating something that *requires action in compliance*, use an Architect's Instruction and make sure that a file of copies is kept and a master list made of the instructions issued for quick reference. *Anon*'s efforts above bring home the importance of dating and numbering them correctly.

It is important that the appropriate administration forms are used for a particular contract, and that they have the latest amendments incorporated or amendments sheets attached. Pads of forms often have far too long a shelf life, and should be regularly checked to make sure that they are current.

Make sure that copies are distributed properly. Whether or not the particular form has a printed box indicating to whom copies should be sent, it is essential to keep the employer, quantity surveyor, appropriate consultants and, where necessary, nominated specialist firms informed. It is equally important that clerks of works receive copies.

Agree with the contractor at the start of a project which are going to be the most efficient lines of communication. To avoid delay, it is often necessary to send copies to the contractor's main office and to the site office. Fax is becoming widely used in the building industry for that reason, but if you fax an architect's instruction to site for quick action, be sure to send the originating AI to the contractor immediately and distribute the copies in the usual way. As its name implies, fax is simply a process for *transmitting a facsimile of an original*; it does not take the place of that original nor does it have an existence in its own right. And be warned – *faxes fade*.

8.4 Employing staff: advertisements, forms, letters

Whether or not you have recently started up in practice on your own, the day may come when you will be responsible for taking on more staff, perhaps a project or trainee architect and/or a secretary. You may need to write advertisements for these appointments, and you will probably need to write a job description for each.

Writing advertisements

Advertisements are part of the process of matching what you need with what others are offering.

The *RIBA Guide to Employment Practice* recommends that a job advertisement should contain:

- the name, address and telephone number of the practice, and the name of the person to contact (alternatively, a box number may be used);
- the title of the job, a brief description of it, and where it is based;
- what attributes a successful applicant is likely to have;
- details of salary (or salary band), hours of work, any special conditions (eg a compulsory contributory pension scheme);
- information on how to apply: by telephone or in writing, and whether to enclose a c.v. and details of portfolio.

The Guide also sets out proper grades and titles of architects' posts. Don't be tempted to make up your own; they may turn out to be contrary to the professional codes or even illegal.

How to 'pitch' the advertisement will depend on what sort of practice yours is and the sort of person you are trying to attract. If you look through the technical press you will see that firms vary widely in this respect. Some talk about themselves as *we* and the applicants as *you* – the friendly approach. Some use the third person throughout: *the successful applicant will be expected to . . . ;* this can be rather off-putting. However, it is possible to be informal without appearing to gush, or formal without seeming cold and autocratic.

If you particularly value design flair and/or a good academic record, then say so. On the other hand, you may put experience at the top of the list. It is reasonable to advertise for these attributes – they are things that can be demonstrated by applicants. To ask for *a self-motivated approach* or *compatibility* is a waste of expensive words; these are things which you will have to judge for yourself when you interview applicants.

Whether you decide on a formal or informal approach, use consistent wording throughout, and make sure that the advertisement is attractive and the information well presented. Many architects prefer to design the layout themselves and include the firm's logo. There is more advice on this subject in a book in this series about public relations.

A job description

However basic the job, it is sensible to write a job description for

FIG 8.2
Job description form

JOB TITLE .... Job No. ....

Office/Department .... Base ....

Summary of duties ....

Detailed duties ....

Special skills/experience needed ....

Special responsibilities ....
(for staff, budget)

Accountable to

(This part for administrative records)

Job title .... No ....

Holder of post ....

Salary .... Start date ....

Any special agreement, review? ....
....

How was post filled?
        (1) by advertisement in ....
            on (date)
        (2) by ....

reference and comparison. Most jobs shift in scope or emphasis over the years and if there is a job description, adjustments to wages and salaries can be related to the recorded facts about the post. The description can also be a point of reference if there is any dispute or grievance. As well as the title, duties and responsibilities of the job and any special responsibilities or projects which are relevant at the time of appointment, the job description should specify to whom the incumbent is accountable. Fig 8.2 illustrates the format required. The details should be updated each time there is a new appointee.

A job description should not be confused with the Written Statement (required under the *Employment Act*) of the main terms and conditions of employment which has to be issued to all full-time employees not later than 13 weeks after they start the employment. Refer to the *RIBA Guide to Employment Practice*.

You could send applicants the job description before they come in for interview, but if your practice is new, you may prefer to draft the description afterwards when you have agreed specific duties with the new member of staff. In any case, the new appointee should be given a copy when he or she starts work.

Compiling a c.v.

Only very large architectural practices have their own application forms, so you will probably ask applicants to write in and enclose a c.v. A well-presented c.v. gives a good impression of the candidate and is also a great help to the interviewer. The *RIBA Guide to Employment Practice* gives example headings, which have been incorporated into a suitable layout as Fig 8.3.

Standing in the shoes of the applicant for a moment, there are also a few commonsense *do's and don'ts* to bear in mind.

Do include details of your secondary education. Employers like to see where you went to school and what O and A levels you obtained. With 1992 approaching, don't forget to mention any ability in a European language.

Don't leave out your age, however sensitive you feel about it. It's a giveaway, and the reader can easily work it out from your career history.

Do begin your career history with details of your present appointment and work backwards. Give dates, job titles and a résumé of duties. Be brief.

123

FIG 8.3
Format for a c.v.

Curriculum vitae

NAME ....

Address ....

Tel no: ....

Date of Birth ....   **Nationality** ....

Education
.   Secondary
      qualifications obtained (give dates)

.   Architectural
      qualifications obtained (give dates)

Work experience (give dates)

.   (begin with most recent)
.
.
.

Membership of professional associations
(specify)

Details of CPD, committee work
(specify)

Other interests
(hobbies, sports, preferred reading etc)

Publications
(details and dates, attach any relevant to this post)

Referees
(work, character - say whether permission to approach them
must be requested)

Do get all important information on to the front page. A lecturer at one of our distinguished schools of architecture gloomily remarked recently that in his opinion architects never read anything longer than a paragraph. Try not to think about that – just pray that he had overstated, not understated, the case.

The second page of the c.v. can include information about the rest of your work experience, your interests and aspirations, and the names of work or character referees. Remember to say whether referees can be approached direct or not, or you may have some explaining to do to a pained employer who is not aware of your intended departure.

When you respond to an advertisement and send in your c.v., write a brief covering letter (Fig 8.4). This is your first chance to make an impression. Be brisk and enthusiastic. Remember to:

- head the letter with the name of the post being advertised;
- say where you saw the advertisement;
- say why you are particularly suited/attracted to the post;
- say you hope to be called in for interview soon.

FIG 8.4
Applying for a job: covering letter with c.v.

Dear Sir

ADVERTISEMENT FOR THE POST OF ...

I would like to apply for this post, which was
advertised in yesterday's **Building Design**. I enclose my
curriculum vitae.

As you will see, I have spent the last three years in
South Wales designing industrial buildings of various
kinds, so that I have a range of experience that seems
to suit the post admirably.
[or]
I have always been impressed by the high quality and
performance of the buildings you design, and this job
would give me an excellent opportunity to broaden my
design experience.

I am available for interview any time, and may be
contacted at the above address. I hope to hear from you
soon.

Yours faithfully

FIG 8.5
Record of interview form

POST

Job title .... Grade/number ....

Date of interview .... Time ....

Interviewer(s) ....

CANDIDATE

Education/training/qualifications
.
.

Experience
.
.

    Reason for applying ....
    Personality ....
    Appearance ....
    Hobbies, interests ....

SUITABILITY

For post
....

General ....

Interviewer's comments ....
.
.

(This part for office records)

Application acknowledged .... (date)
First reply oral/written .... (date)
Second reply oral/written .... (date)

Interview expenses paid   .... (date)

Offered post? (yes/no) ... . (date)
Accepted?   (yes/no) ... . (date)

Interviewing candidates

Once applications have been assessed and shortlisted, the interviewing process begins. It is useful to have a Record of Interview form (on the lines of Fig 8.5) and to jot down information about the applicant during the course of the interview. The headings help to ensure that no important matters are forgotten, and they can be a useful prompt if questions threaten to dry up at the interview.

Immediately after the interview, write down your impressions of the applicant before your judgment (or simply your memory) is clouded by other applicants or by subsequent events. Even if you decide not to employ the interviewee, don't throw away the Record of Interview or any c.v. provided. Many appointments fall through, and second or third best candidates are recalled. Sometimes it turns out that an applicant interviewed for one job is ideal for another.

Letters of appointment, refusal

Letters of appointment should be semi-formal (*Dear Mr — Yours sincerely*) and should refer to the firm as *we*. They should confirm the discussion and agreement reached at the interview(s), and may have attachments such as a contract of employment, and the statutory statement of working conditions. Fig 8.6 is a specimen letter for appointing a clerk of works.

A letter of refusal could look like Fig 8.7. Remember David Rock's advice about being nice to people, even if the interview was a near disaster. There may have gone tomorrow's Minister of Housing.

8.5 Writing references

It is usual to ask permission to offer someone's name as a referee for a specific appointment, but sometimes this is overlooked and it may come as a surprise when the reference is taken up and you have to respond. You may also be asked to write a general reference (Fig 8.8) by a member of your own staff who is leaving to look for a job elsewhere.

When writing references it is important to be fair not only to the ex-colleague or employee but also to the prospective employer. You have a duty to disclose any seriously adverse events or circumstances that occurred during the person's employment. However, matters of personality are a more usual reason for changing jobs. Wherever possible, be generous. *You* may not be sorry to see the person go,

FIG 8.6
Letter to newly appointed clerk of works

Our ref.: BL/HM/Appts89/F
26 June 1989

B Finch Esq
72 Old Common
Wargrave
Berks RG2 8PJ

Dear Mr Finch

APPOINTMENT OF CLERK OF WORKS:
'Treetops' Estate, Chorley

We are pleased to tell you that the employer, (name), has
instructed us to confirm your appointment on the terms
agreed at interview and as described in the enclosed
contract of employment and description of your duties and
authority as clerk of works.

Please read these documents carefully and then sign, date
and return the contract to us in the enclosed envelope. If
there are any matters that you would like to discuss further
before signing the contract, please telephone us.

So that you can familiarise yourself with the project, we
enclose a set of drawings, bills and specifications as
issued to the main contractor.

There is to be an initial project meeting on (date), which
you should attend. An agenda is attached. You will see that
your duties and responsibilities as clerk of works are to be
discussed under (items x and x).

On your first day, please report to the project architect,
(name), at this office, and collect a pad of weekly report
forms, a daily diary, and a pad of Directions.

We hope that you will enjoy your work on the 'Treetops'
project and look forward to your joining us on (date).

Yours sincerely

(name)
Encs
Copy to: (employer)

FIG 8.7
Letter of refusal

Our ref.: BL/HM/Appts89/neg
26 June 1989

B Finch Esq
72 Old Common
Wargrave
Berks RG2 8PJ

Dear Mr Finch

APPOINTMENT OF CLERK OF WORKS:
'Treetops' Estate, Chorley

Thank you for coming in for interview yesterday. I am sorry
to tell you that your application has not been successful.

We were impressed by your knowledge of the building industry
and your interest and enthusiasm, and we will keep you in
mind when and if other appointments are being made.

Yours sincerely

(name)

---

but remember that he or she may 'gel' much better in some other work environment.

General work and character references may be headed *To Whom It May Concern*, and are simple to write if you imagine that you are being asked the following set of questions:

- How long has this person worked for you?
- What posts did he/she hold?
- What is he/she like — as a person?
                       — as a colleague?
                       — as an employee?
- Why did he/she leave your employment?

Employers who ask for a *general* reference are usually mainly concerned to discover whether the person in question is competent, honest and reliable. A prospective employer taking up a reference given on a c.v. will usually write and ask you not only for your general comments but also your view of the person's suitability for the post in question. In that case you will respond thoughtfully and appropriately in a letter.

FIG 8.8
A general reference

From:　　(Partner/Personnel officer etc)

TO WHOM IT MAY CONCERN: ANITA MARY JUDD

Anita Judd worked for this firm for seven years, first as a junior wages clerk and then as General Assistant, Accounts. She was a capable, conscientious and well-liked member of our Accounts staff.

Anita left our firm in 19-- to work abroad. We wish her well.

Signed ....

Date ....

8.6 Quality Assurance

No one who has read up the requirements for quality assurance registration under the international management standard BS 5750: 1987 (ISO 9001) can fail to appreciate the importance it places on a systematic approach to practice management.

'Quality assurance registration' means registration as a firm of assessed capability in a specific field as defined in the Certificate of Registration, with special emphasis on the management aspect. Practices who have decided to prepare for registration are finding it a salutary exercise, requiring a stringent analysis of current practice habits and procedures. It is not an exercise for the faint-hearted. About a year is needed to prepare for assessment and a further year for the assessment and registration procedures to take their course.

To become quality assurance registered architects have to satisfy a recognised assessment body that their project and practice procedures conform with the requirements of the Standard. This 'seal of approval' upon the way a practice operates may give British quality assurance registered architects an important edge over their unregistered competitors when the vast European market opens up in 1992. The Property Services Agency, which itself applies quality systems in some of its design offices, has indicated that by the early 1990s it intends to use only consultants who are quality assurance registered.

Using the proper tools
The requirements of the Standard attach explicit importance, within the context of a quality policy and system, upon:

- initiating and maintaining effective lines and means of communication; and
- recording and disseminating information in a systematic way.

The office manual (see 8.7) plays an essential part in this process as a source and repository of information as well as a vehicle for internal communication.

If you do decide to prepare for registration, you will need to demonstrate that you have and use the appropriate tools. These are the relevant published codes, assessment schedules and reference books.

There is a special list of relevant titles included in the Bibliography at the end of this book, including the *Architect's Job Book*. The fifth edition retains the RIBA *Plan of Work* as a recommended operational framework and consists of two volumes of systematic guidance, checklists, specimen letters and forms associated with job and contract administration. The accompanying *Job Record* is a set of forms specially designed to help architects record essential project information easily and thoroughly. If one set is compiled and completed for each job, there will be visible evidence of systematic job administration.

Other sources of guidance and good practice are the NJCC Codes of Procedure for tendering, and the CPI conventions for a common classification of production information which can be applied through all stages of tender and contract. In the context of quality assurance it is more important than ever to use the JCT standard forms of building contract, which are recognised throughout the building industry, and the associated forms and certificates published by the RIBA.

8.7 An office manual

An office manual tends to come into being willy-nilly when a firm expands and it becomes clear that *somewhere* there needs to be a comprehensive in-house reference document which sets out the firm's structure, philosophy, personnel and procedures, who is responsible for what, what to do in emergencies, and so on.

Apart from its crucial role in establishing and maintaining a quality system, the office manual is an excellent management tool in its own right in that it provides support and guidance for staff, clarifies policies and responsibilities and ensures that working procedures and methods are coordinated and efficient. It also has a useful role as a 'domestic' interpretation of the standard practice guides.

If you are starting up in practice, you can gradually fill up a folder of specimen forms, layouts and so on related to standard procedures and policies, and develop this into an authoritative collection of facts about your firm, including a statement of its philosophy and objectives. Fig 8.9 is a framework for an office manual which was recently used as the basis for a study at one of the principal schools of architecture.

The contents could be arranged looseleaf with card thumbguide dividers in different colours to demarcate important sections. It is important to be able to update and revise the material easily. Large practices are more likely to need a *series* of office manuals, including one which specifically relates to quality assurance procedures. In that case, the divisions shown in the Figure could be assumed to be separate manuals rather than separate sections within one manual.

Writing and keeping the office manual up to date is time-consuming and involves considerable effort, and must be someone's designated responsibility, preferably one of the firm's principals. One or more copies should always be available for reference by all staff.

At its simplest function as a vehicle for internal communication, a well organised, up to date office manual saves an unimaginable amount of time in the long run by providing ready answers to a multitude of everyday queries from staff at all levels.

8.8 Using a personal computer

Many architects bravely decide to start up in practice with only a personal computer and a telephone answering machine to help them.

FIG 8.9
Framework for an office manual

----

1   Structure of the firm

    Legal status
    Date of partnership etc formation
    Names of
        principals and special responsibilities
        solicitors
        accountants
        bankers
        related practices

2   Practice philosophy and policies

    Practice objectives
    Practice structure
    Practice organisation
    Corporate plan
    Practice portfolio

3   Practice development

    Promotion and marketing
        policy and implementation
        responsibilities

    Publicity policy
        image and implementation
        brochures, newsletters, visiting cards etc
        press notices
        public relations

    Staff development
        strategy for practice development
        policy for staff training and monitoring
        CPD

4   Quality control policy
        BS 5750 quality system

(continued)

Fig 8.9 *(continued)*

```
5   Practice control systems

    Information control
    Administration control
         employer's obligations
         Health & Safety at Work requirements
         work allocation and programming
    Financial control
         accounting records
         income and expenditure budgeting and monitoring
         cash flow procedures
         insurance requirements and procedures


6   Project control systems

    Project staffing          Financial
    Information               Technical procedures
    Administration            Project records


7   General office routines

    Security, safety, emergencies
         fire escape, fire fighting
         safety clothing and provisions
    Office support services
         telephones, telex, fax
         copying and printing
    Furniture and fittings
         amenities
    Computers
         policy
         hardware and software
         programming and use
    Maintenance, cleaning, accommodation
    Cars
         purchase, lease, hire
         mileage, maintenance, insurance, taxation
         allocation and use


8   Administrative routines

    Administrative support policy
    Administrative and secretarial procedures and
         responsibilities
    Filing and record systems
    Communications
         policy and procedures
```

(continued)

Fig 8.9 *(continued)*

```
        Project numbering and procedures
        Mail handling procedures
        Filing, records, archives, storage
        Material supplies, stores


9       Staff selection and appointment

        Staffing policy
        Terms of engagement
               working hours, overtime etc
               holidays, sick leave, leave of absence
               notice and termination
               salaries, bonuses, reviews
               pensions
               insurance and safety
               expenses, car allowances etc
               private work and conditions


10      Project planning and costing
        Project records
               collation and analysis of information
        Project planning
               fee assessment and allocation
        Project control
               targets and programmes
               time control
               progress evaluation


11      Technical procedures

        Policy
        Project organisation
               roles and relationships
               staff allocation
               use of consultants and specialists
               appointment procedures
        Survey and briefing procedures
        Design procedures
        Production information procedures
        Drawing record systems
        Standards and preferred procedures, materials,
               suppliers, contractors and sub-contractors
        Forms and documentation
        Programming and progressing procedures
        Site control and administrative arrangements
        Information services
               office libraries and technical information
               project information collation and circulation
```

Life can be testing, to say the least, in the early days of practice, and if you have recently taken up the challenge of 'going solo', perhaps the best advice is to put down this book (temporarily) and go and get a copy of *Starting up in Practice* by Susan Hay. It is practical and encouraging and points you towards many useful sources of information. Then read Jaki Howes' book in this series about buying and using a pc. (Details of both books are given in the Bibliography.) You could also refer to the RIBA *Practice* Supplement 'Computer Update', which was included with the *RIBA Journal* (December/January 1988).

Drafting on the computer

It saves an enormous amount of time and effort if you can get used to drafting letters, reports and minutes on the computer instead of laboriously writing everything out. In this one process you can amend and revise material as much as you like until you achieve a final version, to be printed out with the appropriate headings and references added.

It helps to compile and maintain various lists on disk, and also the minutes of meetings, as the format and headings will stay the same and some minuted items may only need minor amendments. But please *don't* try to invent your own forms for contract administration and on no account 'manufacture' your own forms of contract. The agreed and recognised forms have been devised for the protection as well as the convenience of all the parties concerned, and the smallest of unnoticed errors in a 'home-made' version, such as *not* being typed as *now* could have dire consequences.

The pc is ideal for keeping rapidly changing information up to date, but you will eventually have to print out and file away much of the material as hard copy, because this is the best form for reference and retrieval and allows simultaneous access by a number of people, which a pc does not.

Part 3

Writing texts

Section 9

Short talks

'Curtsey while you're thinking what to say. It saves time.'

(Lewis Carroll)

At some point in your career you may be asked to give a short talk to start off a discussion group or introduce a seminar, or to give a longer talk on a specific topic. The event may be in-house or organised by some committee or learned body associated with the building industry. The texts required differ from those prepared 'cold' for publication in the technical press in that they have to be written, delivered and then used to spark off questions and/or a discussion.

The first task is to write a brief outline of your theme. Then decide how you are going to tackle the topic and jot down principal headings in a logical order.

9.1 Organising visual aids

Your second task is to assemble whatever visual aids you have and decide what others are needed and of what kind (blackboard, slide carousel, overhead projector etc). Then when you begin to write out the talk, you will be able to tag in references to them. Even when your talk consists of mainly visual material with commentary, *always write out what you are going to say.* Even the most experienced speakers can dry up or get distracted on occasion. Always include with the tag in the text a written reminder of what the slide etc shows. Then if the slide fails to come up for some reason, you can blithely tell the audience what they *ought* to be seeing if only you weren't surrounded by incompetent assistants and malfunctioning machinery – although the truth may be that you may have simply failed to press some button yourself in the heat of the moment.

Audiences need a little time to digest new information, so don't put up a visual aid and start talking about it immediately. Pause for a moment or two of digestion. Similarly, they are likely to become confused if you fire slides at them in rapid succession.

9.2 Structuring the text

Organise your text in the usual way – a beginning, a middle and an end. In the case of a talk, the beginning will include salutations, scene-setting and a description of the way you propose to tackle the subject. As ever, the middle will contain the meat of your message, logically organised and developed. The difference comes at the end, as we shall see.

The beginning

It is diplomatic to find out if anyone special will be present to whom you should refer in your opening greetings. The knotty problem of how to address a visiting Monsignore or the Chief Minister of Matabeleland can be unravelled by reference to Debrett's *Correct Form* or Black's *Titles and Forms of Address*, and a quick phone call to the Protocol Department at the Foreign and Commonwealth Office. Otherwise, the usual way to begin is:

GREETINGS
Chairman/Madam Chairman, Ladies and Gentlemen, I am delighted to have this opportunity to talk to you today

SUBJECT
about the growing problem of . . .

CONTEXT
As you know, this topic has received attention in the press recently . . .

STRUCTURE
I am going to begin by . . . then I shall . . . finally, I intend to show that . . .

TIMESCALE
That will only take about 15 minutes, which will leave plenty of time for you to fire questions at me . . .

Never begin by admitting that you have not had enough time to prepare the talk properly, that you have a terrible cold, that the beagle has left you, that this is the first time you have spoken in public. Remember the golden rule:

Stand up, Speak up, and Sit down (soon, preferably).

The middle

As well as organising your message logically, it is a good idea to categorise information into what you *must* say, what you *should* say, and what you *would like* to say, time permitting (it usually doesn't). Don't over-write your talk; keep to the *must* and *should* says, and reserve the *would like* to says for throwing in if you are under-running (unlikely) or to pad out a 'dry' question or discussion period. Always keep an eye on the time; don't over-run by more than about five minutes or you will upset the organisers and any subsequent speakers, and the audience will become restless and won't listen to you anyway. And when you *do* finish, nobody will ask questions in case you start talking again.

The end

Experienced speakers try not to sum up too tidily. Leaving a few strands of thought dangling is an excellent way of teasing out questions and promoting discussion. If there is no chairman, remember not to relax when you have said your piece; it is *your* responsibility to get questions and answers flowing or preside over a final discussion. The sign of a good talk is the lively discussion that follows it.

If possible, do a dry run of the talk, preferably in the room where it is to be given, and time it. Ask a colleague to be your 'audience'. The spectator usually sees more of the game, and his or her comments may be invaluable.

Section 10

Talks for conferences

Talks for conferences usually need to be longer, more formal and to deal with the subject in greater depth, but the same general principles for tackling them hold good. Conference programmes and proceedings are often published, so that you may need to prepare three different texts: an abstract, a full text for publication, and an abbreviated version (lasting about 20 minutes) which you will present and illustrate at the conference. A full discussion (about 30 minutes) of your paper by the delegates usually follows the presentation.

10.1 Writing an abstract

The conference organiser will ask you to provide an abstract of your paper for inclusion in the published programme for the event. Send this in on a separate sheet of paper. Head the abstract with the title of the talk and your name, with appropriate affixes. It should be typed double-spaced. Ask the organiser whether or not it should be written in the third person (*The author will review* . . .) or in a more direct style, and how many words are needed. Fig 10.0 is an (eccentric) example.

10.2 Writing the full text

The organiser may supply special sheets on which the camera-ready version of the full text should be typed up and returned by a given deadline. (Copies of it will be handed to the audience to accompany your presentation on the appointed day.) Instructions will be included about format and presentation and whether diagrams may be included and, if so, at what scale. It is usually possible to add brief references and acknowledgments at the end of the paper.

If you are not one yourself, find a good typist. This is not the time for a d-i-y bodge which may cause your confrères, envious of your learning, to fall about in paroxysms of glee. In any case, the organiser may object.

142

FIG 10.0
An abstract

Infestation by Mortar Spiders: a growing problem
by Peregrine Sparrow DipArch

Fully recovered after his disturbing investigations
into attacks on building site personnel by masonry
bees, Mr Sparrow has recently turned his attention to
the increasing incidence of infestation of church
belfries by mortar spiders.

He will describe his recent survey in the North
Midlands, undertaken to determine what environmental
factors influence the devastating appetite of these
tiny arachnids for weak cement mortar (approx. 1:1:12).

(number of words)

10.3 Writing an abbreviated text

Treat this text as a talk in its own right. Don't assume that the
other delegates have read it; it is better to assume that they haven't,
and take the opportunity to encourage them to do so. You can either
present a résumé of the full text with illustrations, or confine yourself
to detailed consideration of one aspect in particular. If some time has
elapsed since you prepared the paper, it might be appropriate to update
your audience on your own recent work or research being carried out
by others.

Concentrate on making a lively visual presentation to offset the
inevitable length and heaviness of your full text. The goodwill that this
will generate may stand you in good stead when question time begins,
and take the fire out of some of the grilling your audience have in store
for you.

'He talked on for ever: and you wished him to talk
on for ever.'

(William Hazlitt)

Perhaps people were nicer in those days.

Material for publication

When you have become a luminary of the profession, or even before, you may be asked to write a book or supply material to be incorporated into one, or to write an article for the technical press. If your contribution is to be part of a large-scale publication you may be sent briefing notes to help you with matters of approach, style and presentation, or notes about the 'house style' of the publisher. Whatever the commission, it is sensible to ask if there is any guidance available before you start writing.

11.1 Briefing papers

A comprehensive set of briefing papers should include the following items:

- Summary of project.
- Information about editorial policy, structure, and responsibility.
- Notes on style and approach.
- Notes on preparing final copy, with example pages illustrating preferred format and presentation.
- A list of titles and principal authors or contributors.
- Contents lists for titles and/or principal sections.
- Additional briefing notes for the particular contribution being commissioned.

This is the level of information you can expect if you are asked to contribute to a major publishing project. A good set of briefing papers encourages and supports contributors and saves numerous telephone calls back and forth.

11.2 Style and approach

Style cannot be 'prescribed'. If you think in an organised way, the way you express yourself is likely to follow suit. In general, keep paragraphs and sentences short and language simple. Use diagrams, examples and charts where possible. Follow any guidance given about preparing final copy because it is essential to establish some consistency in the way material is supplied, particularly where there are numerous contributors.

Who are your readers?

Have a clear picture of your readers — who they are, what they need, how much they know already (but don't assume *too* much). Avoid being didactic or admonitory; be supportive and encouraging. The advice and information which you have been asked to offer represents your experience, expertise (and manifest success). Its purpose is to enhance the professional competence of readers.

Keep to the point

It is acceptable to draw upon your personal experience (without becoming reminiscent and anecdotal) and to review the state of the particular art with which you are concerned (without uttering vapid generalities), but it is not acceptable to go out on a limb and use the book or article in question as an arena for doing battle with society or fellow practitioners, nor for 'flying kites' within your subject area, unless your editor has specifically invited you to do so.

Be accurate

If you are quoting the opinions of others, be specific. Say who said what, in what circumstances and in which medium. If you are quoting actual text, it must be reproduced accurately and the reference supplied in full. If anything is being omitted this must be indicated. Quotations should be succinct; readers should be directed to study the originals in their complete form.

Finally, there is a vast difference between facts and reported 'facts'. Check that information is correct and sources reliable.

11.3 How to address the readers . . .

Before you begin to write, you will have to decide how you are going to address your readers (who may be your fellow practitioners). This is a difficult decision and it is important to get it right. If what you are writing is to be part of a larger publication, your editor will advise you.

145

... AS 'YOU'? ...

Addressing them as *you* is friendly but must be done with discretion as it can easily become didactic (*You must always* . . .). It then creates a divide between you the author, and them the readers. With that proviso it is probably the most acceptable and effective alternative overall. You are more likely to get the message across by being friendly and persuasive than by being aloof and prescriptive.

... 'THE ARCHITECT'? ...

However, you may prefer to try a less personal approach. If you decide to refer to *the architect*, three undesirable things happen:

- sex rears its ugly head, and *he or shes* and *himself or herselfs* are spawned everywhere;
- your style gets pedantic and
- remote. *The architect* becomes a distant concept rather than a flesh and blood professional person.

... OR 'ARCHITECTS'?

Try using the plural – *Architects*. Less chummy than *you*, but also less bossy, particularly when you feel bound to express some criticism which isn't necessarily true of all architects. And *they* gets round the sexist problem, as discussed in 2.5. *The architect* lives on in forms of contract and books about them, and is appropriate wherever the *role* of the architect is being discussed.

11.4 Assess what you have written

You may already have a favourite technique for testing your written material. If not, a good one to adopt when you have defined a subject area is to draft a series of questions in a logical order and in due course set about answering them. When you think you have finished writing, read the questions again and ask yourself if you have answered them adequately.

11.5 Preparing final copy

In the absence of specific guidance from your editor, the following notes will help you to develop a systematic approach and should improve the consistency and coherence of your copy.

Texts

Supply texts as hard copy even if word-processed. Use one side only of A4 sheets and double spacing throughout. Each page should be numbered and identified. Use treasury tags to keep pages collated. A typical page 'header' could be:

Job Book Vol 1 Draft 2 (8.6.88)   *Page 9*

Most editors will send you an example page showing the layout preferred, but otherwise the following guidance is fairly standard.

MARGINS

Approx 40mm, or one-and-a-half inches, sides, top and bottom. Always allow more rather than less.

HEADINGS

Use 'bold' for headings, and three weightings only:

* *main (bold caps)*
* *shoulder (bold with initial caps)*
* *side (bold, begin text on same line)*

or, if you like, mark headings *A, B, C* and ring them round. Do not underline headings or end them with fullstops.

ITEMISATION

Use bullet points for brief items (not dashes) or *(a), (b), (c)* for alternatives etc, separated by semi-colons.

UNDERLINING

Use only for items that are to be typeset in italics. (Keep 'bold' for headings.) These include words that are emphasised, case law references (*Crumb v. Jellybean 1897*), foreign words and phrases including legal Latin (*force majeure, contra proferentem*), titles of books and periodicals (*The Architects' Journal*), and names of ships (*HMS Morning Sickness*). Sub-titles such as the names of articles, chapter headings should be enclosed in quotes ('Writing in Practice'); names of buildings should have initial caps, no quotes (the Rover's Return).

INSERTS AND SUBSTITUTIONS

Use numbered diamonds for substantial inserts, thus ⟨1⟩ . Type the insert on a separate sheet and mark and number it to correspond with margin note. Use carets to indicate short inserts of new copy written in the margin, thus 2> .

REFERENCES

(a) To other pages, chapters, figs etc: leave space in text for numbers, eg *(see page 00 and Fig 00)*;

(b) To other publications, codes, BSs etc: insert in the text a number for each in round brackets, eg *(1)*, and type up a separate list with corresponding numbers and full details. Reference numbers may become superscripts when typeset.

Avoid numerous footnotes and do not use them for references. A separate list of references is more useful.

QUOTATIONS

(a) *Brief:*
use 'single' quotation marks and indicate breaks thus . . . (3 dots only). Use "double" quotation marks for quotes within quotes.

(b) *Long* (say, more than 2 lines of text):
put into single quotation marks and centre 5 spaces.

NUMBERING SYSTEM

Use a simple numbering system for working purposes, but keep the weight of headings consistent. The numbering system finally adopted is often not decided until late in the editing process.

Preferred writing habits

(often a matter of 'house style')

NUMBERS Write *one* to *ten* as words, *11* onwards as figures. Don't start a sentence with a figure: write it out (or rephrase).

DATES Write thus: *25 September 1983, the 1980s* (no apostrophe).

DIVISIONS Do not divide words at the end of lines or split up dates, names, titles. (May not apply with justified text.)

BRACKETS Use round (parentheses), not square. Square are usually reserved for special technical and editorial purposes.

SHORT FORMS Write without fullstops *RIBA, JCT, BEC, ACA, BBC, ICE* etc. Give full version when each first occurs, immediately giving short form in brackets. Use short form thereafter.

Drawings, figures, tables

Always supply a photocopy of the item at intended finished size to check that any reduction is satisfactory. Use the metric, not the 'imperial system (although the latter is used in the USA).

ABBREVIATIONS
Dwg, Fig, but *Table* and *Example* in full. Refer to charts, diagrams as *Fig.* Keep to these four categories.

ORIGINALS OF DRAWINGS
Supply at twice finished size without captions and legends. Drawings should be executed in black on smooth good quality paper.

CAPTIONS AND LEGENDS
Write captions in on a photocopy to show exactly where they should be placed. Then type them up on a separate sheet and include any special typesetting directions.

Word processing
Many professional people have personal computers at home as well as in the office and are able to supply word-processed copy. Be warned that 'compatibility' is never total and you should check this with the editor, who may ask you to send in a sample disk of some draft copy before you start writing in earnest. You may be asked to keep control key operations (such as tabs) to a minimum.

11.6 Drafts and proofs

A substantial piece of work often requires several drafts. The first establishes general content and approach; the second usually refines content and may be sent out to be read by experts. The third reflects any further adjustments needed after expert assessment and (often prolonged) editorial pruning and shuffling. Depending on the complexity of the subject matter (and the expertise or otherwise of the author) further drafts may be needed. When final copy is agreed, it will be prepared for typesetting. Thereafter, 'drafts' become 'proofs'.

You will probably be sent first proofs to check. Go through them slowly and carefully. *It is the author's responsibility to check that text is correct,* not the publisher's or the printer's. (This is usually stated in the contract between author and publisher.) The printer will usually only accept responsibility for typographical errors. Last minute revisions and alterations will be heavily frowned upon and will be charged to the

FIG 11.0
Proof-correcting marks

INSTRUCTION	TEXT	MARGIN NOTE
Set in capitals	MISS <u>Grebe</u>	caps./
Set in italic	was <u>unsure</u> whether	ital./
Set in roman	this (had) caused	rom./
Set in bold type	the <u>cracks</u>. She	bold
Set in lower case	(THOUGHT) they were	l.c.
No indentation	⌐ due to aircraft, such	⌐
	as the F1–11s out of	
Insert full stop)	Apthorp⟨ [They are all	⨼⊙ n.p.
New paragraph)	very noisy and	
Run on	fly very,	
	low', she said.	run on
Close up	'It's as if they use the	⌣/
Delete	church church spire	⌿
Insert hyphen	as a land/mark.'	⌿
Insert quotation marks	⟨We should complain⟩ said	⟨ ⟩
Insert space	Dr James, waking⟨up suddenly	⟨#
Tranpose	and belhṗing gently.	trs./
Spell out	'Miss (G.) is completely	spell out / Grebe
Leave as set	and absḣolutely right.'	stet/

publisher or author – and re-proofing is expensive. The second set of proofs is usually final. The artwork will be checked by the publisher before it is sent to the printer.

Special symbols are used for marking up manuscripts and proofs. Some publishers send out guidance about this, but Fig 11.0 shows those most commonly used. The BSI issue a full classified list of standard marks for use in copy preparation and proof correction.

Appendix 1

Tricks of the trade

A1.1 Thematic emphasis and focus

The basic sentence is a neutral statement – 'The cat is sitting on the mat'. If you were to follow this with other uncoordinated neutral statements such as 'The dog is in the garden', 'The sun is shining', 'The kettle is boiling', you would have a collection of items of information with no apparent connection and/or significance.

No one writes or speaks like that. Our communication has a theme, which is enhanced by focusing words or phrases and is made coherent by the addition of clues and link words. Each sentence does three things:

- it looks back to what has gone before (ie it is written in context);
- it looks forward to what is coming (ie it anticipates);
- it provokes a hidden question (ie it is constructed so as to lead the text or argument logically onwards).

Take an extract from a report or a newspaper leading article and go through it sentence by sentence, identifying the hidden questions thrown up and seeing whether they are answered. If they are *not*, then there will be a hiccough in the theme development or argument. At such a point the reader feels vaguely dissatisfied and his or her attention may begin to wander. This is because linguistic expectations have been defeated.

We also use a number of devices associated with grammar and syntax to put colour and impact into our speech or writing. We use these devices unconsciously for the most part – they reflect what many consider to be our innate skill in communication. When we speak or write we transpose (*front* or *invert*) elements of the sentence to suit our purpose: we stop and start, pause to throw in some comment or additional information, and we stress or repeat words or phrases. This is what makes the listener or reader sit up and pay attention. Someone once offered Winston Churchill a dull pudding. 'Take it away', he said, 'it has no *theme*!'

Shuffling the syntax

Changes in syntax (the way words are strung together to form sentences) are sometimes inevitable in progressing theme development, but many are preferential – they are devices which we can use at our discretion. If we analyse these 'tricks of the trade', we can use and develop them consciously to good effect when we need to do so. The devices discussed here are particularly valuable in writing as opposed to speech, where communication is assisted by intonation and visual signals of various kinds.

English naturally tends to give weight to the end of a clause, but the front position is important both in attracting attention and because of its juxtaposition with the preceding clause. Therefore it often suits our purpose to shift items from their normal neutral or 'unmarked' position to the front or to the end of the clause or sentence. (The *sentence* and the *clause* are defined in 2.1.)

'I may be in doubt as to what I perceive or what I feel, but I cannot be in any doubt as to their being *my* perceptions and *my* feelings. The suggestion that this headache might not be mine at all but somebody else's is quite nonsensical.'

(A J Ayer)

In the second sentence Ayer might have said *It is quite nonsensical to suggest that this headache might not be mine . . .* By reversing the structure, he gives the sentence end weight and a marked climactic effect. If you reduce what Ayer is saying to essentials, it is *I may doubt x, but I do not doubt y, and to suggest z is nonsense.* He has cleverly used the syntax to emphasise his sense of outrage.

Interpolation

Another interesting device is *interpolation*, also known as *parenthesis*. This is where we bring the sentence to a temporary halt to throw in an off-the-cuff remark, or add something new, or revise or even reinterpret the whole of what we were saying. *Interpolation* is essentially evaluative. The signals used in writing to indicate an intrusion of this kind are usually brackets or dashes. It is interesting that these interruptions do not have any inherent grammar of their own, nor do they affect the grammar of the clause they break into. They are often used deliberately to expose the view of events taken by the writer, as the next extract shows.

'The hand of Mr S Binding must surely have been behind the drafting of the TUC statement of guidance (why not instructions?)

on union political funds. Mr Tom King, the Employment Secretary, has accepted that statement (at least provisionally) as a substitute for legislation ending the practice under which all union members are compelled to pay the political levy to the Labour Party unless they make the effort to "contract out". . . . A number of unions will almost certainly lose the right to collect political funds. . . . It is hard to avoid the conclusion that Mr King's purpose has been to strike a damaging (but not crippling) blow at Labour's finances.'

Interpolation is used to good effect in this passage from a *Guardian* leader. *Why not instructions?* is evaluative; the writer clearly thinks that *a statement of guidance* is a euphemism. *At least provisionally* moderates what precedes it, and so does *but not crippling*.

'The great surprise has been the public quiescence in the face of this disaster. It is, after all, a supremely sensitive issue – or it should be.'

(The Guardian)

Or it should be is not a case of the writer having second thoughts; it is a deliberate thought-provoking and marked device to trigger off discussion of the next topic — that the public simply don't care.

The rhetorical trio

A set of three repeated phrases or constructions, the *rhetorical trio*, much loved by all public speakers and particularly politicians (see *Going for the jugular* in this Appendix), is an excellent way of winding up an audience (and the speaker). You can even take it one step further and have a *rhetorical trio plus*. This passage is from *Radio Times*.

'Koestler attacked constantly what he called *reductionism*, the reduction of the universe and human beings to mere material, mechanical entities. Brian Inglis, his friend, who is the narrator of the Everyman programme, describes this in the terms one would use about a vast campaign. 'On the psychological front', he says, 'he attacked behaviourism. On the biological front, he attacked orthodox Darwinian evolution. On the physics front, he attacked simple materialism. Even on the philosophical front, he attacked logical positivism. He was really the last Renaissance man, the last person with the knowledge to do this. Now everything has become too specialised.'

Brian Inglis, hot on the trail of the *rhetorical trio*, adopts a battle campaign mode of description, and fronts three *fronts* in succession (watch out for the puns). He then clearly becomes aware that a military commander's operations are usually *quadri*partite – there is a front, a rear and two flanks. So the trio of *fronts* fronted is extended to include a fourth: *Even on the philosophical front* . . . .

Tacking on a fourth element in this way should be reserved for special climactic occasions; its impact derives from the way it upsets grammatical and thematic expectations. Use it where your theme 'peaks out', and remember that it will be impossible for whatever follows to be anything other than subsidiary. In the extract above, the reader gets the strong impression that Inglis' valedictory remarks are slipping away downhill.

These are just a few of the tricks of language which we can use to get our message across in relatively straightforward communication. Now for a brief analysis of something special.

A1.2 Going for the jugular

Have you ever suspected that you were being got at by a political speech? Well, rest assured, you were. Here is the text of a short party political broadcast on BBC 1 by Margaret Thatcher at 9 pm on 7 June 1983. Polling day for the general election was imminent. Bear in mind as you read it that in rhetoric the magic number is three, and the magic ingredient is repetition.

'The choice at this election is crucial. It's about the very nature of the country in which our children will grow up. And it really is a very clear choice. It's a choice between a steady, sensible and resolute government – a Conservative government – and an extreme and erratic opposition which I believe is totally alien to the character of the British people. It's a choice between a Conservative Party which is dedicated to safeguarding peace with freedom and justice, and a Labour Party which would weaken our defences and undermine NATO. It's a choice between a Conservative Party which believes in liberty, independence and home ownership and a Labour Party which openly proclaims its faith in socialist control.

At this election we have a chance to banish for ever the dark divisive clouds of extreme left-wing socialism and, ladies and gentlemen, we must take that chance. This is a great country. We are a great people. Together we can do great things if we rise to the challenge of our times. We ask you to renew our mandate with a clear decision and a resounding majority on Thursday.'

When you have recovered from the effect of those heavy hammer blows of contrived linguistics, you might like to analyse the utterances of this formidable lady (and her speech writer).

The approach is apparently straightforward. Much use is made of lexical repetition. *The choice at . . . , . . . clear choice,* then three sentences beginning *It's a choice between . . . .* The same construction is repeated in all three pairs of comparisons of what the Tories and Labour are respectively offering the electorate.

Look at the contrasts in the three sentences:

TORIES	LABOUR
• *steady, sensible resolute*	• *extreme, erratic, alien*
• *dedicated to safeguarding peace with freedom and justice*	• *would weaken defences, undermine NATO*
• *belief in liberty, independence, home ownership*	• *faith in socialist control*

The contrast between Tory *belief* and Socialist *faith* is subtle but damning. Faith, like love, is often blind, whilst belief has a sound base in knowledge. Here it is belief about warm, cosy things, as opposed to faith in something apparently cold and nasty.

Choice then becomes *chance* (just two letters change) and we have a pair of clauses *We have a chance . . .* and *. . . we must take that chance.* Another trio of sentences is grouped around the adjective *great: This is a great country. We are a great people. Together we can do great things. . . .*

Note the switch to *we* in the second half of the text, where Mrs Thatcher begins to wind up her audience, and the *ladies and gentlemen* interpolation to make sure we are all paying attention before *We must take that chance.*

Then into the home straight. The *we* that meant you the voters and we the Conservative Party changes finally to *we the Conservatives* who are asking *you the voters* to renew *our* mandate. By this time listeners are no longer aware of the difference between *you* and *we* — they're hooked! The last two words before Mrs Thatcher relaxes her verbal stranglehold are a reminder that Thursday is polling day.

So ends a straightforward message about choices, chances, challenges and final greatness. Or so it seems. What the lady is really saying is this:

You and your children are under threat! The Socialists are coming. They are extreme, erratic and alien — they could do *anything*! You *know* they are going to weaken the country's defences and undermine NATO. You are going to be part of a society that is controlled by blind Socialist dogma. What can you do? Vote Conservative and get rid of them for good!

Mrs Thatcher's *real* message is all about fear.

But if you stop and think about it, most advertising (for that is what party politicals are) is to do with making people afraid. If you don't use this toothpaste your teeth will drop out, if you don't drink a certain brand of vermouth or drive a certain make of car you will be a nobody, if you don't use this washing powder your children will be ridiculed, if you don't telephone your granny you'll make her cry and so on.

And if you don't read this book? Well, that *would* be a pity.

Appendix 2

Toujours la politesse

As discussed in 5.6, the information given in this Appendix is strictly limited to the formalities of writing French business correspondence and assumes some knowledge of French. Little has been published in the United Kingdom on the subject, but two useful titles (published in France) are included in the Bibliography. It will be no surprise that they are in French.

A2.1 How to write the date

Dates are written
le 14 juin 1988

Sometimes the city or town is repeated from the address, eg
Paris le 5 septembre 1988

Notice the *le*, and that months are usually written without initial capital letters.

A2.2 How to write the address

Write the addressee's name as
Monsieur HULOT Claude or *Monsieur Hulot*
followed by his business title.

The French still generally prefer the 'old-fashioned' indented layout for their letters, and put the recipient's name and address top *right* on their notepaper. We more usually adopt the blocked-to-the-left style, which *they* refer to as *la méthode américaine*.

EXAMPLES:

(a) *Monsieur HULOT Claude*
95 avenue du Prince Orange
1180 Bruxelles
Belgique

(b) *Monsieur Hulot*
Directeur d'Administration
CEMENTOSIS S.A.
67 cours des Juilliottes
76892 Paris Cedex 17
France

Roads, streets, avenues etc are written without initial capital letters, and the district code precedes the town or city. *Cedex* (Courrier d'Enterprise à Distribution Exceptionelle) plus a number is a code for a special delivery service. *S.A.* stands for 'Société Anonyme', *S.A.R.L.* for 'Société à responsabilité limitée'. When addressing evelopes, you can abbreviate *avenue* to *av., place* to *pl., rue* to *r.* etc.

A2.3 How to address the intended recipient

The point about getting the opening greeting right is that it puts the reader into a suitably receptive frame of mind. The French are sensitive about this.

(a) Formally
If you do not know the recipient personally, begin
Monsieur or *Madame/Mademoiselle*

as appropriate or, if you are writing to an organisation
Messieurs/Mesdames (ie plural)

Use *Madame* where you do not know the marital status of a lady (but see (c) below).

(b) Informally
Friends and colleagues may be addressed
Cher Ami, Cher Collègue, Cher Monsieur, Chere Cécile

Don't add the family name: address your French bank manager Pierre Hulot (who you hope is your friend) as
Cher Monsieur not *Cher Monsieur Hulot.*

(c) Officials
Some officials, notably lawyers (*notaires, avocats, avoués*) like to be addressed as *Maître*. Address a judge as *Monsieur le Juge.*

Members of the Administration like to be addressed by their titles, eg
Monsieur le Préfet,

heads of service as
Monsieur le Directeur, Monsieur l'Architecte en Chef,
Monsieur le Percepteur (tax inspector) etc.

But beware if the incumbent is female, because many titles remain masculine nonetheless. For example, a lady judge is *Madame le Juge*, and an Under-Secretary of State is *Madame le Sous-Secrétaire d'Etat*. A 'female' title such *Madame la Ministre* simply indicates that a woman is *married* to Monsieur le Ministre.

A2.4 How to begin the letter

After successfully leaping the hurdle of the opening greeting, the next obstacle facing you is how to begin the body of the letter. There is an ultra-polite 'rule' that you should avoid beginning with *Je* or *Nous* as the recipient may reasonably be expecting that, after addressing him or her so felicitously, you are going to *talk* about him or her. This may force you into the passive:

Votre lettre de . . . nous est bien parvenue . . .

However, after a correct greeting you are unlikely to give offence by getting straight to the point. Here are some typical openers in order of formality:

Nous accusons réception de . . . (We acknowledge receipt of)
Nous avons bien reçu votre lettre de . . . (ditto, but more friendly)
Nous vous remercions de votre lettre de . . . (Thank you for your letter of)

A2.5 How to continue

Veuillez trouver ci-joint/ci-inclus nos plans, lettres de contrat. (Please find attached/enclosed our drawings, letters of agreement.)
Nous vous confirmons que . . . (We confirm that . . .)
Comme suite à notre entretien . . . (Following our discussion . . .)
En ce qui concerne le/la . . . (With reference to . . .)

Notice how the polite French use the subjunctive *veuillez* of the verb *vouloir*, often in final greetings. It is the equivalent of *Would you be kind enough to . . .*

Never use the second person singular *tu* in business correspondence; this is only appropriate between close friends, and within the family group.

A2.6 How to end

If you have requested something in the body of the letter, it is polite to thank the addressee in advance for the trouble this will put them to. You could say:

Vous remerciant à l'avance de votre diligence (trouble) *et de votre bonne collaboration* (cooperation) or *Nous vous remercions d'avance de . . . .*

Note that although we thank people *for* something, the French follow *merci* and *remercier* with *de* (of).

If someone has to sign a letter for you in your absence, the usual formula preceding their signature is:
Pour M. Sparrow et sur ordre.

A2.7 The final greeting

You will be fairly safe if you adopt the formulae set out below. Occasions for going over the top and offering *mille remerciments* (a thousand thanks) are rare in business; in any case, in a continuing correspondence it is best to take your tone from the last letter received.

(a) Formal
The standard formal final greeting is:
Veuillez agréer, Monsieur, nos salutations distinguées.

Safe, anonymous but rather old-fashioned. It could be varied to:
Nous vous prions d'agréer, Messieurs/Mesdames, nos salutations devouées.

Another formal variation is:
Veuillez croire, Madame, à l'assurance de nos sentiments les meilleurs.

(b) To a client
A formal letter accepting commission could end:

En vous remerciant pour la confiance que vous nous témoignez, nous vous prions d'agréer, Monsieur, l'assurance de nos sentiments devouées.

(c) Among professionals
The French are especially fond of addressing one another as *Cher Collègue* even if the writer is an architect and the recipient a marine biologist. As well as the opening greeting, this might be included as part of the graceful exit:

. . . d'agréer, Cher Collègue, mes salutations distinguées.

(d) Oui, Monsieur le Ministre!
A letter to, say, the Chief Architect of a Préfecture should conclude:

Nous vous prions d'agréer, Monsieur l'Architecte en Chef, l'assurance de notre haute consideration.

To someone of even dizzier importance, such as the Minister of Housing, your *consideration* should become *très haute.*

Similarly with the clergy. A Mother Superior could expect:

l'assurance de nos sentiments respectueux,

whilst an Archbishop, in spite of knowing the burning consequences of spiritual pride, will be content with nothing less than your

sentiments profondément respectueux.

Funny as it all may seem, to the people in question this pecking order of politeness is important.

A2.8 Remember the accents

French is full of them, and they sound rather like symptoms of disease: grave, acute and circumflex. Some words, such as *garçon*, even sprout cedillas. If you have gone to the trouble of composing a letter in French it is worthwhile going through the typed version and inserting the accents by hand if the typewriter or word processor is unable to do it for you.

A2.9 French numerals

On drawings, remember to cross your *seven*, thus: 7 , so that it is not confused with *one* which, French-style, looks like this: 1 .

Note also that the French use a comma where we use a decimal point, eg

1,75F is one franc 75 centimes, and
6,421 is six point four two one, whereas
6.421 is six thousand four hundred and twenty one

Exasperating as it may seem, the French themselves are not keen on writing letters. It is said that this is because of the bruising years they spend at school struggling with the grammatical intricacies of written French. Made so acutely aware of the beauty of their difficult language, they will only write it when they have time to write it perfectly – and that isn't often. So don't be surprised if they seem to prefer using the telephone, however bad your spoken French is.

Bibliography

1 General

English Grammar Today: A new introduction
  by G Leech, M Deuchar and R Hoogenraad, Macmillan 1982
Sociolinguistics
  by P Trudgill, Penguin Books 1974
Stylistics
  by G W Turner, Penguin Books 1973
The Business of Architectural Practice
  by D Sharp, Collins 1986
The Central Questions of Philosophy
  by A J Ayer, Penguin Books 1973
The Complete Plain Words
  by Sir E Gowers, revised by S Greenbaum and J Whitcut, Penguin Books 1987
The Expert Witness and his Evidence
  by M P Reynolds, P S D King, BSP Professional Books 1988
Towards a Contextual Grammar of English
  by E Winter, Allen and Unwin 1982

2 Books published by RIBA Publications

These may be obtained off the shelf from RIBA Bookshops at:
  66 Portland Place, London W1;
  35 King Street, Bristol;
  113–15 Portland Street, Manchester,
  or by mail order from:
  RIBA Publications Ltd, Finsbury Mission, Moreland Street, London EC1V 8BB;
  (telephone 01–251 0791)
Architect's Job Book
  compiled by L Beaven, S Cox, D Dry, R Males, Fifth edition, 1988
Architecture and the Principle of Harmony
  by P F Smith, 1987
Choosing a Computer (provisional title)
  by Jaki Howes, (forthcoming)
Dissertation Handbook
  by P Willis, 1983
Public Relations in Practice (provisional title)
  by Fenella Gentleman, (forthcoming)
RIBA Guide to Employment Practice, 1987
RIBA Handbook of Architectural Practice
  (New part-work edition to be published in 1989)
Starting up in Practice
  by Susan Hay, 1987

3 Titles relevant to Quality Assurance
(available from RIBA Publications)

Architect's Job Book (see 2 above)
RIBA Plan of work for design team operation
   (reprinted from the RIBA Handbook, 1973 edition)
The NJCC Codes of Procedure:
   (those directly related to the *Architect's Job Book*)
      For Single Stage Selective Tendering
      For Two Stage Selective Tendering
      For Selective Tendering for Design and Build
      Procedure Note 15: Commissioning and Testing
      Procedure Note 16: 'Record' ('as fitted') Drawings and Operation and
      Maintenance
The CPI documents of coordinated conventions, especially:
      Production Drawings, a code of procedure for building works
      Project Specification, a code of procedure for building works
      National Building Specification (subscription service)
Architect's Appointment
   (with the latest fee scales amendment) 1982
RIBA Handbook of Architectural Practice (see 2 above)
JCT Standard Forms of Building Contract
   (Full list from RIBA Publications.)

It may also be helpful to refer to:
   RIBA Guidelines for Sound Practice
   RIBA Examinations in Architecture
   Code of Professional Conduct

   Relevant *Practice* Supplements

4 Titles published in France

La Nouvelle Corréspondance Privée
   by Yann Delacote, Editions de Vecchi, Paris 1987
Le Grand Livre de la Corréspondance Commercial et d'Affaires
   by Francois Pouthier, Editions de Vecchi, Paris 1986

Index

References are to sections, sub-sections, Figures and Diagrams (D1, D2 etc).

Index

Index